ake up this
make it right
ve to make
t.

respect each

h other so

o dictator can

estroy one

er de wereld
zelf

NIETS ?

世界の平和が続くために

六の一　鈴木　尚枝

みんなが一生懸命働いているのに
貧しい人と、富んだ人がいるのだと
日本は今、たいへん不平等だと思
う。貧しい人もいるし、大富豪もいます
不平等をどうしたら、平等にできるの
ぼくは考えます。
わが国では、富んだ人は大都市
ます。また、貧しい人も、その人た
りようとして、大都市に集まってた
と思います。

Σοφία Κρπιειιοϋ
«Τί θα έκανα νά διορθ
ιιώόρειο»
Άν έγώ κυβερνούσα τόν
θά ήθελα τά παιδιά νά
τούς γονείς τους, τά γρα
σταματήσουν νά δουλεύουν.

Cher Monde Moderm

En effet, c'est en vu de la situation actuelle qu
ne mon regard vers toi. Te rends-tu compte d
se passe au sein de ton peuple? Le titre glorie
t'es donné, me fait peur lorsque je considèr
qui se fait au dedans de toi!
Quand j'avais l'âge de dix ans, j'étais ton me
et souvent je courais ~~derrie~~ derrière les dive

ville ønsk

alle Husse

de blomster
Taget. og at

ikke var nogle

ikker og biller,

at alle

var

Dear World

'How I'd put the world right' ~ by the children of over 50 nations

Edited by Richard & Helen Exley

Methuen Toronto New York London Sydney

Acknowledgements

The editors would like to thank the many schools and teaching staff who helped in the creation of this book, and the children for all their boundless enthusiasm. Our thanks go to Oxfam and to the many personal and publishing friends who helped with contacts in different parts of the world, and to the London embassies of many nations who helped to secure the co-operation of their educational authorities.

We would like to thank the *New Internationalist* for the entries from Sierra Leone and Norway. Also, Desclée de Brouwer for the choice of French entries and Wendy Coupland who showed us the many beautiful pieces of writing from the children of Wales.
Finally our thanks go to our friend Eric Evans for his design advice.
Front cover drawing by
Boeru Daniela Lucia, 13, Romania.

By the same editors;
The Missionary Myth (1973)
Grandmas & Grandpas (1975)
To Dad (1976)
To Mum (1976)
Happy Families (1977)
What is A Husband? (1977)
DOGS (and other funny furries) (1978)
CATS (and other crazy cuddlies) (1978)

First published 1978
by Exley Publications Ltd, Watford, England

© Exley Publications Ltd 1978

This edition published in the United States by Methuen, Inc., 733 Third Avenue, New York, 10017 and in Canada by Methuen Publications, 2330 Midland Avenue, Agincourt, Ontario, MIS 1P7
LCCCN 78-20852
ISBN 0-458-93940-4

Published in Australia 1979
by Methuen of Australia Pty Ltd
301 Kent Street, Sydney

National Library of Australia
Cataloguing-in-Publication data is as follows:
Dear World
ISBN 0 454 00132 0
1. Children's writings. 2. Drawing.
I. Exley, Richard, ed. II. Exley, Helen, joint ed.
808.8

Printed in Spain by Graficromo.

Teachers and educational authorities from every country in the world were invited to participate in the creation of *Dear World*. The final book is the work of children from over 50 countries ranging from Haiti to Japan, and from Finland to New Zealand. The children were asked to tell adults how they would put the world right. The answers, as might be expected, are often passionate, sometimes full of hope, and sometimes deep despair. They have the innocence and charm of childhood, and a compelling honesty. Some come from children with all too much experience of the problems they are writing about; the child from Cyprus whose mother was killed in war, a former street urchin in Colombia writing about orphans, the coloured child from Canada writing about racial prejudice.

Spelling and grammar has not been changed, except where this has been essential to make the meaning clear. Every word in the book, and all the drawings, are by the children.

This is a book that all adults, and perhaps especially all politicians, should read. Some of the entries may be heady, idealistic, maddeningly impracticable. But coming through the words there is a theme, and it's full of hope for a gentler, better world.

Richard & Helen Exley

Vicky de la Calva, 10, Spain

4

We are young people
We come from countries all over the
world
We believe in different gods but
We can join our hands and rebuild a
peaceful world

Lefki Silvestrou, 17, Cyprus

We, the children of the world, are the
ones who suffer most when there are
wars. Our elders let hate rule their
lives and we who wish only to love
each other are taught to hate others.

Gerald Hoyte, 10, Trinidad

The world is like a crystal ball ready
to smash into pieces at any moment.
We, the young generation,
hold the ball in our hands.
We mustn't let it crash.
We can bring love and peace.
We can fight for this. We can keep
the ball still. Well, let's fight.
We are holding the world in our hands.
We can stop war and hate and bring
back the missing love.
Yes, we can, because life and the
world belong to us.

Josephides Panayiota, 17, Cyprus

why can't children rule the world.

*Karen Hamilton, 7,
United Kingdom*

If I was a high standing person in the world, I would put the children in charge.
Maybe they would do it better than the grown-ups, and working against war and the injustice they would make the world live in peace, love and justice.
Marinou Panayiota, 14, Cyprus

Little children don't know how to hate. They love everybody. They don't care if somebody is black or white, rich or poor.
When we start to grow up, we learn how to kill, how people fight each other to take more for themselves. So we begin to hate, and love only ourselves.
When we are grown ups we change our feelings and we don't love the people as we did when we were kids.
We do anything to have a good life and we don't care about the problems of other people. Sometimes we like to help them, but sometimes we don't care as much as we should.
If we continue like this, we'll destroy our life, our beautiful world and we'll stay alone without friends, without help.
But, of course we can save the world if we stop making war, hating each other, fighting and killing people.
We can save the world if we live with justice, peace and love.
Why don't we try it?
Symeou Maria, 15, Cyprus

Anat Blum

There are many nations in the world — hundreds of them. Every nation has its language, habits and manners. But one thing — and I think its very exciting — is common to all the nations: the children all over the world are the same. It doesn't matter whether they are black or white, whether they come from the east or the west, they stay what they are — simple kids, all the same, that know nothing about nations and races. The children all over the world have the same games — they play with marbles, they play football (in one way or another), and they are so friendly. I think that if children were ruling the world, there would be no problems like we have today.
Anat Blum, Israel

I am a school girl. I am fifteen years old and I am thinking of the future. For, I think that at the age of fifteen, one doesn't belong anymore to the protected world of childhood, that innocent world where one thinks one knows everything. No, it is not the truth. We must open our eyes to reality. Our parents are not always models of good nature, virtue, or of love. But what will I myself be like later?
For now, it is not possible to hide myself from the children who die of hunger, or how rare happy people are, or that war is idiotic. Today I am thinking of the future.
Christine, 15, France

To Children of the World

Graveyards: this word can become a reality as helpless, we look at the armaments against us. All children regardless of their colour, world outlook, and religion — feel hunger, pain and suffering equally.

So, together, we must stop the wave of evil which carries in its wake destruction of the world.

We cannot live without ideals, without solidarity and confidence in ourselves, without mutual trust.

No! We do not want to live in fear and insecurity for each coming day.

If we want to be happy we have to climb over the wall of evil and hatred, we have to be united in brotherhood and believe in ourselves. Children of the world! Lets hold hands and push evil off the Earth.

Ewa Suplacz, 15, Poland

Living in a world torn by conflicts, in a world where the poor fight against the rich and the exploited against their exploiters, the young are always aware of these conflicts and their effect on the social and economic development of their continents. As future leaders they feel obliged to play an important part in the solution of these problems *now*, so that tomorrow's world may be free from the tensions of today's world. Why are they not given an opportunity to implement their ideas, as this would not only give them a feeling of pride in contributing to world progress, but would also prepare them for the tasks that lie ahead of them. In most cases, what the young generation gets is frustration of their ambitions

In our search for solutions, let us not forget youth — on which we can rely for the continuation of the struggle until victory is won, since the future belongs to the young.

That is my message to the world.

Moagabo K M Mathiba, 19, Botswana

Adults should take more intrests in children and listen to what they say. Quite a lot of children have some good ideas, but, if children were to rule the world it may go well for a while but then children would then begin to get worried about things and not be able to cope with such a weight on their shoulders.

Hannah Smith, 11, Australia

I know what you're thinking, that I'm just a silly little girl who doesn't know a thing about Politics or the world, but I know what I can hear and see and I hate it. So start thinking - Now.

Donna Banyard, 13, United Kingdom

I believe in peace not war. The world would be different without crime. I also believe in no drugs. No smoking as well. I also think kids should have a go at being Prime Minister and things like that. I think sport should be played for fun, not for money.

Angus F. Bathgate, 11, Australia

A Jensen, 9, Denmark

Dear Friends of the World

Let's come together to set the world right. Let's unite. Let's be one. Let's become different atoms of the same liquid and then freeze to become a solid — harder than diamonds and rarer than Californium. Don't think that this is impossible. As Robart Godard says, 'It is difficult to say what is impossible in the world. The dream of yesterday is the hope of today and the reality of tomorrow ...'
This is not one man's job as I am not Lincoln or Gandhi, but it is the work of whole of mankind. It is the work of me, you and he. So, the brains of the world, let's combine to form a nation of nations.

Sanjiv M Mehta, 15, India

If men wanted to join hands,
There would not be a single soul
  who was hungry,
If men decided to love each other,
There would be no more misery
  and justice would reign.
If every man wanted to try to be
  brothers,
Brothers in thought,
The Universe could change
And the world would be a place
  ruled by God.

*Margareth Cazeau, 16,
Haiti*

Island and mountain, sunshine and
  breeze,
Flowers and moonlight, swaying palm
  trees,
Forest and river, white coral sand,
This is my country, this is my land.

Dark were the days when men lived in
  fear,
Fear of the arrow, stone club and spear.
Darkness too deep to quite
  understand,
That was my country that was my land.

Though we are children, soon we will
  be
Teachers and leaders of our country.
We'll build Fiji now as God has
  planned,
Make this his country, make this his
  land.

So shall our country be free and strong,
Homes filled with love
  bring laughter and song,
Peace in our hearts and work for our
  hands.
Fiji united with other lands.
Fiji united with other lands.

Sayeda Banu, 13, Fiji

I will root out the egoism of myself, my country, my people. I will try to develop the thinking of oneness. There will be no caste, creed, religion. I will make them to feel in a way that they are the citizens of the world and they belong to mankind.

G Meena Rani, India

*I would like to see
no more hunger
Killing, greed
or pain.
Because this world
we live in
Has everything
to gain.*

*By working
all together,
By linking body
and mind
All through out
the land
For the sake
of all mankind.*

*Marian Lea, 11,
United Kingdom*

Neftu Ovidiu, 12, Romania

Chorus of the World

If you look around
You can hear a sound
Of a great big chorus's song
It is not of sadness
It is not of badness
It's of love, and it's never wrong.

Every mouth sings it loud
Every man is very proud
He is singing
   in the chorus of the world.
All the nations sing together
All the people now are gathered
To sing the song
   about a nation of the world.

Anat Blum, Israel

Kirsikka Saalas, 16, Finland

Sanjiv

Let's magnify our feelings and let's stretch our love. Let's love honestly without any deceit. Let's love now without any reservation and change the earth from a battle-field into an abode of love.

Sanjiv M Mehta, 15, India

If we are satisfied with what we have, and dont grudge people, we'll be better off because all of this leads up to an unclear heart. With an unclear heart things like killing, shooting and robbing come in mind. If we exercise a little more love this world would be a better place.

Judith Holmes, 14, Jamaica

Love never fails
And is the source of truth,
Love is patient
And can endure all things.
Love is not selfish
But bears all that life brings.
Above all, love is hope,
For without it, we are doomed.

Joy E D Webster, 16, Barbados

I think that a difficult life, war, poverty, and hunger are human mistakes which exist because of the selfishness and greed of some people and nations. In other words they exist simply because there is a little word we always forget. This word is 'LOVE'. Love is not a word to be pronounced; it is a moral feeling which exists in ourselves. This simple word is the secret of existence and the continuity of life.

Abdel Megid Iman, 15, Egypt

If we all love each other the world would change and people would be smiling as they pass by. When you love each other you feel that you are in a place where there is peace. The people who need your love are the sick, poor and the lonely.
There is a time for sharing, giving, loving and a time when you must be kind and good and not selfish.

Andrea Richardson, 9, Trinidad

This exquisitely formed being — whose 'mind is restless, turbulent, as difficult to subdue as the wind' — is desperate. In spite of all his faults, his crimes and his vices, man is still in need of one of the simplest and easiest solutions, a solution that does not need any material means, no money, no weapons; a solution that knows no colour or race; that does not distinguish between king and beggar, between young or old. This solution is composed of four easy and uncomplicated letters, L-O-V-E, love.

Laila Risgallah, 19, Egypt

**The world is just a great big onion, there is time for tears, but yet no time
for peace. And the only way to break free, from this big onion,
is to Love, Love, Love, you and me.**

**People, listen to what I am saying, don't you know we must be free?
Can't you see the penalty we're paying
don't you know what its got to be?**

**If we put this big onion, into a cooking pot,
and season it with peace and love let me tell you what we've got**

**We've got love and unity,
We've got friendly togetherness
We've got lots of happiness
For the world is just a great big onion, waiting – just waiting to be free.**

Cheryl Worrell, 17, Barbados

Yesim Erdesözer, 15, Turkey ▷

Love

We all need love. We, from boy to man, from male to female, youth to old people, love is a must. Nobody on earth can remove love; love is like an iron pillar; we cannot move it. If we possess love, we won't fight.

Suppose a boy, by mistake, uses bad words and the other fellow catches hold of him, beats him and scolds him even if the first boy asks his friend to forgive him. Why does he beat him? Because, he has no love towards his friend. If he has real love towards him, he will at once forgive him; that sort of boy, because of love, will shine in his future life. But he who even in spite of asking pardon, refuses to forgive, is really a brute; there is no love in him. He is not a man. He is not a human being. You may be a lakhier, wealthy richman, what you need first is love. Don't try to be a man of wealth, don't wish to be a rich man, don't wish to possess crores and crores of rupees! Try to love others! That, you should really wish! If you wish to be a wealthy man, first of all you get a good job. Then you can earn money. But love you need not search and get. You can get love in any place, on travelling, on your seat, on a journey, anywhere you may find love.

Paul Raj, 13, India

Our earth is so beautiful,
God made it so,
With our tall trees, our deep sea
Our blue skies and our wildest of
     flowers.
Yes, our world is beautiful,
If we would only stop and see
But we could make it better in
     the split second of an hour.
If we would only love our brothers.

Marie Scott, 14, Jamaica

Adje UgbarUgba, 11, Nigeria

12

It would be good, a stupendous happy-go-lucky place if every soul loved each other. What would happen to the world if we all loved each other? The flowers may never cease blooming, there will always be a smile present on the lips of each human being. The cats will purr, the monkeys will crack jokes and the dog's will laugh!!

You may all remember experiencing a small, small hot argument with your jealous, jealous friend. At the same time you may remember a big, big cat-dog outburst with your neighbour just because your innocent dog had chewed off the end of the neighbour's cat's tail. All these heart-breaking, embarrassing and unnecessary actions will never take place if there was love in each soul, instead of nasty and nefarious thoughts.

Espionage, forgery, murder, crime would never have been practised or even dreamt of, if this world had pure love. A pistol, an automatic pistol. What is it's basic use? To kill, to shoot at first sight — why, because you hate the culprit. Weapons like guns are mainly made to kill a person, to destroy god-given life.

Nowadays it is wise to give a second thought of going out alone in the evenings, especially in the case of females. Horrid thoughts like, 'Will I be safe or get robbed', 'What if I get raped', will circulate in the mind. The reason is because the world is sick and lacks the vitamin 'love' desperately.

Meherina Khan, Fiji

Peace and love should become symbols of the whole world. Then our world will become like a big nice garden full of green trees, and happily playing children. The nice and innocent smile on a child's face will appear once more, such a nice smile we've been deprived of since love disappeared from our hearts.

Wars are like swords in the hearts of little children. I assure you that the minute love returns to our lives and opens our hearts big smiles will appear on our faces. Happiness, tenderness, peace and hope will fill our hearts again. Then the world will be heaven on earth.

Nelly Nabih Youssef, 17, Egypt

All of us have problems. But it's not necessary to fight in order to solve these problems. With love everything would be perfect.

But what is love? Love isn't a beautiful dress or an expensive present. Love is your help to the person who needs it. Love is a smile to all the people around. Love must fill our hearts every year, every day, every moment.

Love can win war. We must destroy the guns. And when we do this, when we fight with love, when we stop the game with fire, then our world would be a better world — a world without wars, without poverty and pain.

Please smile, to bring happiness.
Please love, to make earth a globe full of love.

Eleni Kyprianou, 15, Cyprus

If we all Loved each other We would not fight. We would hold hands. We would share.

Ramdaye Singh, 5, Trinidad

Paivi Herno, 16, Finland

13

If I ruled the world I would make the world look pretty. I would paint the world gay and bright and I would make the houses blue, yellow, green and red and make the garden fences pink or brown or pink, yellow, green, red, blue and white or brown like the rainbow.

Angela Harrington, 8

If I had to put the world right I would have all lamp posts, letter boxes and phone boxes painted different colours like yellow and orange so that people can see them easily.
To make houses nice to look at, I would make them like Tudor houses with beams and beautiful doors and windows and each garden to be big.
If I had to make things easy for people to get around I would invent some sort of moving pavements going round like a conveyor belt with one for each road.

Sylvia Pipon, 11, United Kingdom

'Let's see a more
colourful world' by
Dilek Durmaz, 14,
Turkey

If the world was a picture I would take a painter's brush and I would turn the wars into festivals, the thorny wire nettings into rosy wire nettings, I would turn darkness into light and hate into love.

Hadjissava Elena, 14, Cyprus

If I ruled the world, I would teach, and be wise and noble.
I think my world would be indeed changed from a dust-bin to a heaven. My world would be as bright as a button, as clean as a new pin, as gay as larks, as friendly as a puppy, and peace shall be as 'continuous as the stars that shine and twinkle on the Milky Way, and it will stretch along the margin of each bay.'

Jennifer Douglas, 11, Trinidad & Tobago

If I owned the world I'd stop the greedeness. I'd keep it free from wars and squables. I would let peace live in it. I'd let the black and white live together. I'd let everybody go to heaven and leave hell way behind. The black stairs will collapse and the golden stairs rebuilt.

Michael Kennedy, 10, New Zealand

War is death and destruction,
It is not only the people that get hurt!!
Flora and fauna on the battle field get more injured than anyone.
So . . .
I would stop war and invent other solutions to arguments.
And . . .
I would make everybody even in wealth and food,
And . . .
I would make people less cruel to **themselves, animals and plants.**

Richard Wilson, 10, Australia

I would like to have little country lanes with sparkling fountains going along it, so you can walk along them at night.

Tracy Johnson, 11, United Kingdom

**I dream of a world,
Where men live in freedom's peace,
A beautiful world.**

**I dream of a world,
Where flowers grow unchoked,
Beasts naturally.**

**I dream of a world,
Where everyone has time,
Time for you and me.**

Sonia Gill, 13, Barbados

When I dream of the perfect world I think of a world free of air and water pollution. What a great world it would be if it was made up of lush green paddocks, everyone would be happy. There would be no war or no starving children, everyone would be loved and cared for. Little animals would come out of there burrows and run freely.

I dream of sky's blue as blue and coloured birds everywere, I dream of coloured fish, and corals different sizes, and love filling the air. That is how I'd like my world to be — no hatred just love, kindness and happiness.

Elwyn Mellick, 10, Australia

Hale Kandemir, 15, Turkey

17

Dreams

*Arthur
Yeong Chong Sen*

Sarah Hughes

Tonight

Tonight I had a peculiar dream. I dreamed of you, my dear world. It was a very exciting but a very beautiful, a wonderful dream.

I'll tell you: the newspapers, TV and the radio proclaimed nothing but good news. The responsible politicians refused to declare war. They found a way to reconciliation.

No crooked finger on the trigger release, no thunder of guns; no angry hand using a scalpel.

Bombs forgot to explode.

Generals decided to play golf instead of leading an army; hurting, slanderous words stayed pressed behind the lips; dictators opened the prisons.

Dissedents were respected.

People of all races had equal rights; the frontiers between east and west were opened; conversations took place in a friendly atmosphere.

People began to tell the truth; they allowed adversaries to come close to their thoughts; they found compromises which satisfied workers and employers.

Sometimes they even smiled about themselves; they started a new life.

And you yourself, my dear world, you looked so fresh, so young; the air surrounding you was pure and refreshing; your springwater was sparkling clear; sap-green meadows, murmuring woods, high snow-covered mountains, dreaming lakes and deep, wide, clear seas decorated you.

No pollution; animals full of energy; treasures of all kinds hidden inside you … I couldn't imagine something more beautiful than you.

It was so nice to see all kinds of living creatures so happy and so full of life; it was a visionary view.

Suddenly I awoke and knew — it was not reality, it was just a dream, a dream of a better world.

Elisabeth Katzensteiner, 17, Austria

An awful night for TV

It was an awful night for television so I went to bed early. I got to sleep immediately and soon found myself in a wonderful dream. I dreamt that I was in a better world earth. The air was clear and the sky was blue much better than the fume choked air of today. All the people were a light tan colour like they had all been on holiday. Everyone was smiling even the frail old folk who could hardly move. This was because they were taken care of properly. The food tins were transparent so the people could make sure the food wasn't bad before they bought it.

The houses were all very grand and everyone had the same size so that no-one was jealous. All received equal pay and they didn't have to pay income tax. Children only went to school for three days in the week. Each month they had a week off school. It was Summer all the time so people wore swim suits all the time.

There were clubs and bars all over the world for young children but they didn't sell alcohol in fact no one sold it. All the ladies were pretty and all the men handsome.

In each town there was a television station and the children put on the programmes of their choice.

When I woke up I expected to find myself in this better world but of course I was in grotty London.

Sarah Hughes, 11, United Kingdom

When your dreams don't come true
Don't cry
Be happy
Because when you're happy
Life is a dream too beautiful to dream.

Marion Visscher, 15, Netherlands

One morning

One morning I went outdoors for my routine exercises. I took a deep breath and was amazed because the air was so wonderfully fresh. There was not a trace of pollution. Everywhere birds chirped away in dulcet tones. Had it not been for the alluring aroma of my breakfast cooking and the obligation to go to work, I could have stayed in the garden the whole day.

I poured over my morning papers as I ate my breakfast. I nearly choked when I read the headlines — 'Cost of Petrol Reduced 50%'. I could hardly believe my eyes.

On my way to work, more surprises lay in store for me. A total stranger on the street greeted me and I actually saw a man pick up a scrap of paper and throw it into the dust bin; a rare sight indeed. The local florist, notorious for his parsimony, pinned a carnation on my lapel. 'Free of charge, saudara', he added with an amicable grin. As I strolled along, I noticed that everyone seemed to be in a merry mood — smiles lit up their usually sullen faces. Passing the news-stand I saw, 'Famine in India overcome', 'Pollution — no longer a threat to mankind', 'Drug abuse — practically non-existent', etc, etc. Feeling tremendously elated, I muttered a prayer of thanks.

I quickened my pace as I approached my office because I was already fifteen minutes late. Entering the office, I sensed an atmosphere of serenity instead of the usual hustle and bustle. My manager, who was a martinet and who was very particular about punctuality, did not hit the ceiling as I had expected. On the contrary, he patted my back and said, 'It's such a beautiful day why don't you take the day off and go fishing or something?' 'I b..beg your pardon sir?', I stammered in response. After thanking him, I half ran out of the office, secretly thinking that my manager ought to be sent for a psycho-analysis.

Going home, I crossed the river that meanders through my town. Its murky waters were now crystal-clear and the fishes were swimming so temptingly near the surface that I dashed home to fetch my fishing gear.

I said to myself, 'I must be the happiest man alive'. At that precise moment, I pinched myself — just to make sure that all these were not a dream. I pinched my cheek hard and … and it did not hurt. It *was* a dream!

Oh! Why must it be a dream?

Arthur Yeong Chong Sen, 16, Malaysia

Pia-Leena Kettunen, 14, Finland

19

Suk Bal, 12, India

Once I was dreaming that I was building nice houses so that the world will be nicer. I would like to change the world into a big garden so all of us will be able to play in it. And in the house a big swimming pool to swim hundreds and hundreds of klomiters. The shops would not cost anything. The king would come to see us incas we are sick. We would be fre if we did somthing rong. But we had to say sory. And the world wars would not exist. And the animals could speak in cas they were hungry and lots of other things.

My name is
Yvonne
Schlubach, 9,
Spain

I wish this world
would be happy,
And everybody
would sing and
shout.
Everyone would be
kind and never
kill or steal.

Animals and birds
would be free
to run about.
And in their own
kind of way they'd
sing and shout.
Simone Walton, 11

21

Craina Valentin, 18, Romania

War is the concentration of all human crimes. It turns man into a beast of prey.

Edna Daley, 16, Jamaica

The politicians seem to believe in the sentence: 'If you want peace, prepare for war.'

Pils Sigrid, 17, Austria

Why on earth, do we have war! Money for war but none to feed the poor.

Cheryl Workell, 17, Barbados

Dear Modern World,
When I was ten, I was your best friend, your name had a special sound. But what a shock when I understood — at fourteen, what you meant by 'Modern World'.
'I am very well modernized', you told me, 'since I took my flight from the bow to the machine-gun, and from the machine-gun to the atomic bomb.' You are perfectly right, dear Modern World — you are modernized to shed more blood! Oh! Turn away from that eternal destruction towards which you are going, with stooped shoulders. You have lost so much human blood; lift up your eyes to your Creator.

Namihanla Yonli, 14, Upper Volta

War in this century of ours can be started by a simple order by a superior. It is fought by political figures and not by men.
War is shown in films as an event where anyone who returns is a hero. To many, war is a source of wealth. War is not shown as a thing where millions of people are killed or maimed for life. War is played as a game. It even has a set of rules known as the Geneva Convention.

Stephen MacCharles, 13, Canada

Never, ever, peace
Peace, perfect peace,
No wars, no guns,
Everyone friendly,
An impossibility.
There will always be guns,
Always be war.
If only there were peace.
In a church there is peace.
If the world were like that,
Just think,
How happy you would be,
Knowing that you're safe,
From a war,
From bombs,
From unnatural death.
But, it couldn't last,
There'll always be fighting,
Always arguments,
Always guns,
Always bombs,
Always tanks,
Always war,
But never, ever,
Peace.

Ian Hoare, 12

It was a lovely summer day like all the others that mighty God spares to all his people on earth.
On this cursed day I happen to be on this terrible scene. I woke up by a terrible noise. It was a napalm bomb that exploded in the garden of the house where we stayed.
We began running and huge fires were burning everything. I thought that I was in hell.
But we found refuge in a small cave. I don't want to think what I was hearing. Cries from children who were asking for their parents, women to cry for their husbands, children. Death was passing all over.
When night came we walked and walked. We passed mountains, we walked for hours and at last we were safe.
But behind us we left persons that we will never see again.
Why are people so cruel?
I pray to God so that one day we shall be able to live again in peace, without fear, without nightmares.

Margaret Danou, 11, Cyprus

Since the old times mankind continues to live with hate, wars, suspicion. No country on this earth has managed to keep peace throughout its history. Man is one of the biggest and worst beasts in the world, and in order to show his power always creates wars and a series of troubles.

Ploussiou Annita, 14, Cyprus

The breathless expanse of red-
    coloured smoke,
Slowly beginning to fill the sky,
Hateful and wonderful nuclear war
The birds choke in it and die.
People stand, father, son, peasant
    and king,
A friend beside a friend
Watching slowly, wonderingly,
    without regret,
While for them the 20th century is
    brought to an end
For them life no longer matters,
It is from others, that life should
    not be torn,
They pray the bomb will be banished
From the futures of those not
    yet born.

Misery and hate will flourish,
As millions already know,
That until this bomb ceases to exist,
The horror of war and death will
    grow.
Banish this bomb.
And a small part of peace will be
    restored,
For the price it's costing mankind,
Is far more than we can ever afford.

Mary Vaux, 15, Iran

Constantinou Costas, 18, Cyprus

23

No-one really likes war,
Only kids playing soldiers on the floor,
But they don't know what its like,
Playing aeroplanes on their bikes.

War is a game of strength,
Surviving for months in a trench,
I don't see why men fight,
Because they mostly pay with their life.

Terry Glanfield, 11, United Kingdom

Lincoln, 6

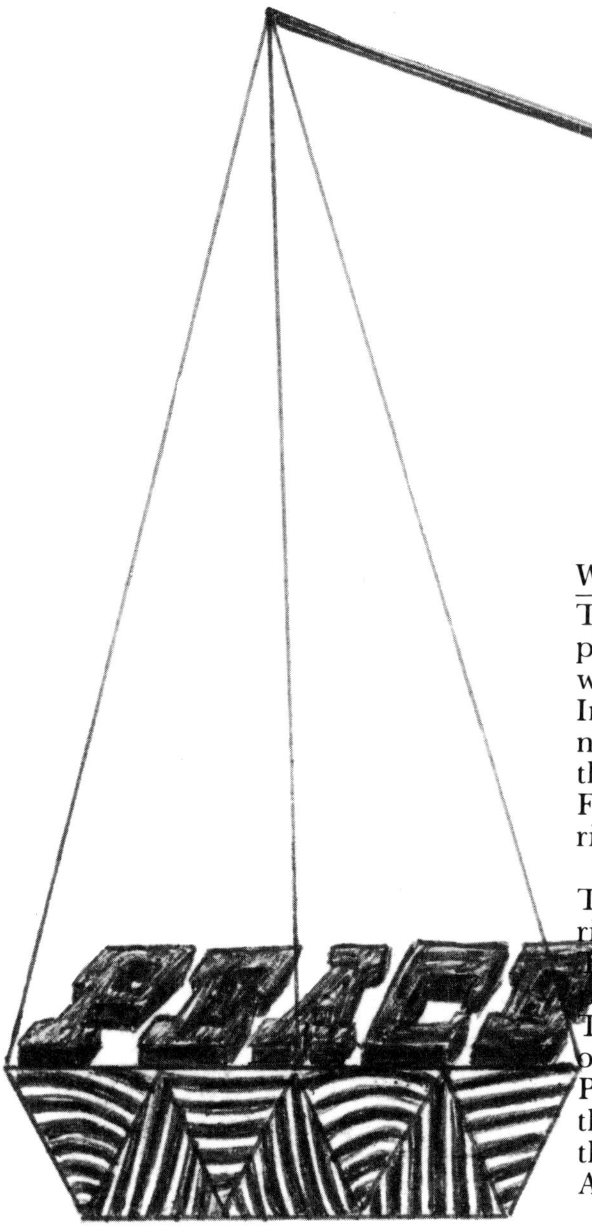

Who pays the price?
The old General,
playing his game,
with live toy soldiers.
In a world of make believe,
not figuring on the fact,
that lives are being lost.
Full of pride,
right up to his epaulettes.

Then there's the officer,
riding on his white stallion.
The horse, like him,
perfect in looks.
The officer is
one track minded.
Promotion is the word,
the only word,
the important word.
Anything for that word.

Then there's the soldier,
musket clasped in his hand,
charging into battle,
plunging into the foe.
Bold and hard as a brick,
Brave as a charging bull,
obedient as a child.

These periodical mass-murders which
destroy so much life and property and
turn men into beasts, must stop. If after
every twenty years of uneasy prosperity
we have a gigantic war, I would much
rather not have prosperity.

Vimla, Fiji

He's dead now.
He paid the price,
of the old general's pride,
and he's promoted the officer.
The soldier is the under-dog.
Or is he?
A wife without a husband.
Children missing a dad.
A mother's lost her son.
They paid the price
of the old general's pride,
the promoted officer.
They did.
They did.

If I ruled the world war would never start and peace would never end.

Brett Hayde, 11, New Zealand

Lincoln Exley

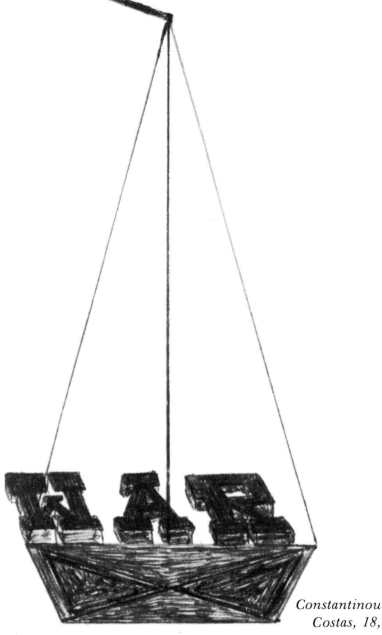

One should be able to go to rest at nights without thinking of who will be attacking one's peacefulness. We need more Kissingers.

Angela Fagan, 16, Jamaica

Since time began, as far as my adolescent mind can remember, there has been hate.
As far back as my memory can go I can hear nothing but war, yes, war.
War, how it rings in my ears. I am far from war but the sound is near and I shall never be the same.
Let us unite, no more wars, let there be memories of war, but none present.
Oh to know that the sounds of explosions will never again be heard.
Oh to know that the only thing to fly in the sky is an innocent bird and not a bomber plane.

Patricia St Hill, 17, Barbados

Let us not make any mistake, the Third World War will be the most destructive and the most permanent in its effects. The prevention of this holocaust lies in the good sense of the peoples of the world to prevent massive rearmament which in turn increases the chances of a tragic war. Action should be taken *now* and not *tomorrow*.
Long live the peoples of the world!
Long live Mother Earth.

Metlhaetsile Leepile, 19, Botswana

Constantinou Costas, 18, Cyprus

History is usually the story of wars between countries. I wish it could be the story of great friendships between countries.

Nedim Üzey, 13, Turkey

I was happy, I had a lovely house, with a nice garden. Everything was smiling to me. Then the Turkish invasion came. There, where happiness was king now came the disaster. The war cut off the wings of happiness and now I am a poor, miserable child, without a home, refugee in my own country, living in a miserable tent.
Why do people are so bad? What wrong did we the children do to them?
I never felt fear and now when I hear the noise of a car or an aeroplane I tremble like the leaves of a tree.
Oh mighty God, help that my poor island, find again the peace. And you blessed dove, symbol of peace, come and bring us again freedom, peace and love among people. We don't ask you for much.

Irene Poyiatzi, 10, Cyprus

The universal language that is understood nowadays is that of guns and pistols. Oh world! I am ashamed of you! People think themselves bold and courageous to kill. It is now an honour for people to kill one another. Where are you, pity? I cannot find you in this big world. All pity has died out because people have grown so used to cruelty. World, I am not blaming you, but it is the fault of those who are inventing things against the welfare of humanity. Equipments of war have increased, atomic bombs have been invented. I really think that those who invent such things are selfish. All they think about is fame or wealth. Why don't we become builders instead of murderers? Why don't people invent things which would make the whole world benefit by them.
In our world, we want people who have principles. Honour is hard to be found. Many suffer from internal conflict. They are torn between keeping their principles, or deceiving themselves in order to adapt themselves to the conditions surrounding them.
Everyone must dominate his worldly needs, including money, goods, pleasure ... etc.

Farouk Manal, 15, Egypt

Andreas Eleutheriou, 15

People have been kicked out of their own native countries. Imperialism, wars, racial discrimination, and social injustice have spread among the nations like a huge giant octupus lying at the bottom of the sea grasping with its numerous arms the little weak fish.

Ismail Hala, 15, Egypt

I do not purport to represent the Israeli youth but I want to declare in the name of the common aim of all teenagers in Israel who will be called to serve their people and country, in the army, in the coming year: The Israeli youth, holds out both its hands, to peace.
The key for an entire understanding is given not to single men, but to the future rulers of Israel and her neighbours: The present youth of the Middle East.
I call my friends, beyond the barbed fences and the mine-fields to demonstrate their real and truthful wish for peace and their hate of the bloody wars in which so many good fellows fell.
Friends! we have a common chance. Do not let it slip away. We have to try everything to succeed where our parents failed.
In my dreams I see no guns, no tanks, no fire. If we try hard we'll win!
Good luck and Shalom.

Arnon Hirsch, Israel

'Cypriot mothers anxiously awaiting the return of their children who did not return from the war.'

*Georgiou, 10
Cyprus*

War: A child's way to peace

I would like to stop people from fighting and having wars. You could take the children from both countries and put them in the middle and then they would not shoot. I do not like the wars. People get killed. Some children get their mummys and daddys killed.

Yvette Austin, 8

We can say to the enemy we are not going to make war by arms but by word because God hasn't given us a heart to hate ourselves hands in order to slaughter each other, he has made us to help ourselves and others.

Haddioui Hassan, 16, Morocco

Oh, if there were no guns and bombs, I'm sure we would have more cheerful chums.

Sharon Gibson, 14, Jamaica

Mr War
Haven't you understood yet that you're a foolish thing? People don't want to cry, anymore. Children don't want to hear about you, anymore. Everybody wants to have a world full of happiness. And our children must live better than us, so you must go. Please let the peace stay in the world forever.
And I call your attention! This is a letter of threat!

Dilek Tasan, 13, Turkey

If I ruled the world I would stop all the wars by putting children in the middle of them.

Gary Sheehan, 9

In my home where I live The Tongan people share and give so what do you think we always have ????
Peace is the word we always gave to people who argues and fights with rage.

I wish, I wish we always have

⋆ PEACE! ⋆

Duane Harris, 11, Tonga

I would like to stop wars. This is how I would do it. I would try to make people learn the good things about the people they have fought or are going to fight.
Alison Gatland, 9, Belgium

If I had the strength to change the world, I would hold a child in front of the people and the child's love and purity would make the people understand how small they are in front of it.
Georgiou Eliana, 14, Cyprus

To put the world right,
it would take millions of years
but, with a little help from mankind
we could make it.

To do all this,
the world needs your help
so please try
and help a little towards world peace.
Amanda Parsons, 14, Iran

I think it is wrong to fight wars, the only wars that should be fought are peaceful ones.
John, 11, Wales

I would prer that thare would not be a world war again and if thare is any other war please do not let many people get hurt.
Stephen, 7, Belgium

Dear World,
Why do people have wars? I think it is usually over money or a thing. A thing is a thing. Why fight over it? Usually the problem can be worked out without a war. Besides, when you have a war over something you usually lose money, not gaining anything.
Sincerely,
Someone who knows
Aldie Ludlow, USA

I would make peace in the world by letting all the soldiers decide whether they should go out to fight or not since the people who decide to go out and fight another country are the people who stay behind in offices.
Joseph Ikageng Nwako, 18, Botswana

I would go to the wars. I wold have a white ink gun. I will put white all the flags. Then the soldiers of the wars will be friends. If two boys were enemyes by a toy car I will buy another car.
Pablo Rodriguez, 9, Spain

Greta Miettinen, 16, Finland

Lynne Fordham, 7, United Kingdom

The only warfare there would be is, a word war.

Helen Green, United Kingdom

I don't like the war because people get killed. I hope there are no more wars. Countries should get along well. If one country wanted some land they could just ask. And they might give them some.

Bruce Turner, 8, Canada

To stop bombing in Ireland, make licorice bombs so that when they exploded, bits of licorice would come out.

Sarah Woolston, 11

BOMBS, BOMBS, BOMBS
The menace of the lot
I would throw everyone of them
into an old junk plot.

And as I lie in bed
I wonder what each day will bring
(sigh).
And I keep wondering what it would be like
If I could make the world go right.

Johnathan Hurrell, 11, Tonga

If only I could stand somewhere and call loudly 'stop the war'. We want peace and love, stop making guns. I want to make men free. We are all brothers and sisters, why are we quarreling? Why do the states make guns?

Zoe Papageorgiou, 16, Cyprus

But I think the thing that is terrible to us all is quite easy to solve. War, is that terrible thing that we all hate, well if we did not have any money and we did not have to pay for thing, but just take them their would be no such thing as war because their would be nothing to fight about and no one would be robbed because you could just walk into a shop and take what you wanted and if you stopped making weapons there would be nothing to fight with and if you kept peace and gave everybody what they wanted there would be nothing to fight about.

Matthew Barry, 9

I would abolish boundaries, so that the wars would come to an end.

Nikos Stelakis, 9, Greece

Build a brick wall between the countries that are fighting.

Amanda Leon, United Kingdom

The way I'd rule the world
I'm just about to tell
To fill the world with gladness
to hide away the wars
down holes and up chimney pots
I'd hide away the lot

Paula Hackett, 11, United Kingdom

If I was the Queen of this land I would tell men that they are not to use guns or knives because you kill people. People do not like it. Children get killed. Just sometimes fathers and mothers get killed and their children have to live with their nanny and grandads or their aunts and uncles or their next door. Or if they have got a big brother or sister that are not at school they can look after them.
But they must not be left on their own.

Angela Harrington, 8, United Kingdom

People should not fight each other because it is only a loss of lives and it is not funny or a sport.

Kerry, 11

I do not like people fighting wars against each other, I think it is very dull.

Catherine, 11, United Kingdom

In the countrys where bombs go off I would make them stop it or els I would bomb them.

Sandra Ludman, 10, United Kingdom

Dear President Carter,
If somehow we could stop religion, that would stop quite a lot of wars, but unfortuneatly not the main war that threatens us. That war is the one between Russia and America. Both countries, as you know, issue atomic bombs. It would be a tragedy if one of those was to go off. A good way to stop this is to have a big ring, in which eleven men of each of the two countries would be fighting to kill. The country that wins will have won the war with only eleven men dead.
Yours sincerely
John

John Downes, 11

There is bombs all over Ireland. People are moving away from Ireland. They do not like the noise.

Mieka Waugh, 9

I will stop the fighting in Africa, in South Africa and in other countries and send doctors and nurses to give plasters to the people and make them better.

Stuart Harpin, 8

I would try to stop wars by bombers dropping bombs on bomb factories.

Andrew Clark, 9

The measure we can take to make peace or to stop war is to bring the two sides and discuss the problem in order to find a solution. If there isn't a solution — *find it by force.*

El Jaadi Abdelmalek, 15, Morocco

I would get some monsters from another planet or make som robots that could go against humanity because then we would all go against them.

Christian Poulsen, 13, Denmark

Bar the sale of newkiller weapons

Stewart Lewis, 11, United Kingdom

I shall make a choclate factory. Choclate flowers and choclate evreything. So the children can enjoy themselfs.

Philippa Oxford, 9

I would make everybody happy all the time (including me sometimes).

Lynn Bachelor, 8, United Kingdom

I think that all laws must be rewritten from the begining. This is what I would do if I ruled the world for a while. I would start everything from the begining.

Margarita Lianopoulou, 8, Greece

I would say, 'I don't want pollution, no factores should throw their litter into the rivers and kill the plants, and living things. And if that was true I would jump and scream 'World you did what I said, I love you World'.

Ana Mari Woehr, 9, Spain

34

For a start we would have to have new criket selectors. The people say we need a new team but we need a new set of selectors the same gose for football as well like Italy they might frash us to hell.

Bild a ship like the Germans Bismark so if the Icelandic fish industry think they can be clever and send out their best 2 gun boats they got disjroid in two shots we could have a ship blown two smitharens. I dont know what the world come to I just dont know.

Matthew Burnett, 9, United Kingdom

If I ruled the world I would make every country talk Spanish and English.
I would make the animals speak.
I would make esear trees to clim, and swimming pools two hundred meters deep, and five thousand meters wide.
I would do a feast every day, and real cars for boys, and not have to sit beside girls in school.
I would make comics of one million pages and donkeys to fly.
I would make girls go mad and boys not.
I would make people die with five million years old. I would make in all schools in the world the teachers not to worrie when some body has broken a leg or have a purple eye.
I would make mums let us have at home parrots, elephants, lions, dogs, cats, girafs, zebras, horses, monkys, etc, etc, etc.

Andres Bayonas, 9½, Spain

If I were to put the world right I would make everywhere shiny and bright. Streets, roads and pavements looking quite in order.
Everyone's face looking bright with wonder.

Lorraine Taylor, 14, Jamaica

I would like my people to live in new houses so that they will not fall down easily. The houses should be made with stone blocks and should last a long time.

Alusanatu Koroma, 15, Sierra Leone

Now about all the men who keep on striking I would give them up to £400 a week and that I should think would please them. And if that didn't please them I would think they were greedy and put them to working instead of putting them to prison. I would only put them to prison if I really needed to.

Louise Miller, 8

I would make sure that the ladies do not do all the housework and let the men get the sore backs, hands and feet.

Eileen McDermott, 11

Dear People,
I have been made a ruler over you, but I'm not the best one among you. If I am just ... help me, and if I am a tyrant, depose me. Those who are weak are strong to me, until I give them their rights, and those who are strong are weak, until I take those rights from them....

Shahin Zeinab, Egypt

Eva Silver, 7

Make all the pyramids square
Do things like that everywhere
Make all the teachers stand still
Make them kiss my feet when they
    kneel
Get rid of schools
And make more swimming pools
Make cars into horses and trailers
Make more ships for the sailors
Make the criminals stop gagging
Make all mums stop nagging.
O! I wish I could put the world right.
Alison Ward, 11, United Kingdom

To put the world right I would make
people make TV's what could show
Tarzan and Batman at the same time.
Paul Howard, United Kingdom

If I was ruler of the world, when the
people started to fight I would say three
times stop that and if they don't I will
hang them because I do not like
fighting.
Abigail McMinnies, 7, Belgium

If I was a ruler I would change the
months in the year I would change
August to the top and April to the
second top January to the third top and
all the other months in the sameway.
Jennifer French, 6½, Belgium

If I ruled the world
School dinners'd be nice
Without lumpy potato
And gungy rice.
Catherine Cockings, 12

If they let me rule the world, I would try
to rub out all social differences among
people.
Mariana Bernitsa, 12, Greece

If I were a soldier I would not kill
enybody because kill is a very nasty
thing another thing I would not like
are the earthenkwate because the stones
will fall in peoples head and that
people will dide and the dide is the
thing that I abolish and another thing
that I abolis is that my mother have to
waik my up when I want to sleep.
Carlos Navarro, 9, Spain

If I could rule the world for a day
These are the things I would like
    to say
Peace should reign all over the land
And money should be thrown out of
    every hand
For money is the cause of every hassle
Wherever it may be, in a hut or a castle
I would look for a planet
Where we could dwell
So the children of our world
Could be free to yell
If I could have ruled the world
    for a day
These are the things I would have
    had to say.
Corinne Rowlands, 12 Australia

If I ruled the world, I would make
happy my people and I would be happy
myself. I would have much money and
I would travel to all places of the world.
Yes, I would like very much to be the
ruler of the world.
Nikos Andreadis, 8, Greece

If can change the world I would give to
the poor people food, and to dont be
any Politics and all can go to schools to
work and all the Fathers can work and
the mothers can buy shoes for the boys
and clothes and trouses and toys and in
all the world the people is civilated and
in the world can reign the peace.
Antonio Aguila, 10, Spain

I would send a letter to all the cuntris I could. And tell them some of the rulls what they should do. I would tell them not to rec enything. And not to bracke enything. or stele enything. And triy to stop the volcanoes erupting.

James, 7, United Kingdom

I would put the world right by putting the price of food down and the price of horses down. Cigarettes will be put up to £2.50p a packet with four cigarettes in each packet. The queen shall no longer be queen. My mother shall become queen. Then the world will be put right. We will get the money by the new queen throwing out money. The law will be broke and new rules will come. No-one shall have their own way. To many people in the world have their own way. I think too many people get away with it, their to dum and idle bone lazy. And a horse will be given two sugar lumps every day. People should have a new queen nearly every year because one queen might be very very kind and soppy and a queen should'nt be very very kind. She should be strict and a little bit kind. The End.

Michelle Le-Clercq

I will make that the mothers of all countries down't have to lous their hands working kleaning the houses. I will make that the cientifik men will invent a robot to do the work of the mothers. After, I will make a house in each countrie for the pour men and women for eat and live. After, I will get off the wor and put pice. And after, I will sit in my favorit chair and wach TV.

Javier Manzarveiria, 11, Spain

A thing of which I am in favour of is that Rugby should be made the National Sport of each country that way it would toughen up all of the weeds and weaklings who sit around during games.

M Davis, 14, United Kingdom

Bryony Eedy, 7, United Kingdom

Dear World...

Dear World,
How are you? I am very well. I would like to see all the good things you have and have fun. I think your nicest part of all is Disney land. Did you see your friend Venus?
Don't you get dizzy of going round twenty four hours?
A lot of embraces of
Deana

Deana Jubert Fischel, Spain

Dear World,
I think the world shound be changed in many ways like boys bigger than everyone beat you up. Fighting shound stop.
Yous sincerly
Andrew Clark

Andrew Clark, 8

Dear World,
I hope you are having a very nice time. If there is anything I can do for you I would be very gratefull to do it, and I would like to stop little children from fighting by telling one of the boys to thump the other boy on the nose and then tell the other boy to thump the boy that thumped him first and then they will hurt each other so much then they won't fight any more.
Yours sincerely,
Glyn

Glyn Jones, 8

Dear Government,

Dear Government I would like to help you very much But I can't help you because I am still in School But when I grow-up I might.
love from Sara

Sara June Clark, 7, United Kingdom

Dear World,
I would put you right by kicking all the priministers out, and giving all the tramps and poor people money, and putting everything down in price and knock all the prisons down, and stop all the wars and find a cure for rabbies and breed all the rare animals and make people love animals.
from Elvin

Elvin Dipple, 8

Bog Walk P.O.
Bog Walk Secondary School
St. Catherine
Jamaica W.I.
The Leaders of The World,
Dear Sir/Madam,
May I suggest sir/madam that instead of some of the many world leaders organising programmes socially, economically and disciplinary they should first organise these programmes for themselves. They should be aware of the fact that blinds can and will in no way lead the blind successfully.
Yours faithfully,
Glenville Bryan.

Glenville Bryan, Jamaica

Dear World,
Your present state is not too good. Nothing but peanut mad presidents in the USA. Bribes and scandals in Spain with frequent changes of primeminister in Japan, and who can forget the black and white mix-up in South Africa. Really world I think something ought to be done about this terrible muddlement. Every evening at 5.50 I hear the news headlines: Man murdered in Belfast by masked gunmen. The only country seemed to be settled are Russia and they are preparing for a war on the west. Why should Iceland argue with Great Britain over a few fish who would rather stay in the sea anyway! In any case I don't like fish much and I'm sure many others don't.
Yours Faithfully
Sean

Sean Moran, 11, United Kingdom

Dear World
I wold like you to change the prices of food and uther things to becase they are too dear. I want you to make the sun shine so we can play and sun bathe. My grass is too long and I want it to be suny so that I can cut the grass.
Love from
Jane XX

Jane Castle, 8

38

Dear Administrators of the World,
I have the request to you to not let the children of the world be hopeless, let them not be stained with hunger, let not their natural laughter be dried up. Please arrange such a rule for us that we can grow with all the children of the world with equal and full bloom. Let not the children hide their face in the lap of their mother,
Yours ever
Sailen

Sailen Ch Shee, India

Dear World,
I wish there were no wars anywhere
And no fear and no suffering,
But you don't take that into account,
    my world.
Dear world, you don't see, you don't
    hear.
Do you know how people are starving?
Have you seen the children in India?
Yes, you have.
Dear world, why don't you do
    anything?
Why don't we help?
My world, how indifferent we are.
But why should I bother about you.
I want to be happy.
Dear world, why should I be
    troubled with your problems?
Do as you deem best.
There's a good film on TV
and I must go and make a sandwich.
Päivi Salmela, 15, Finland

Dear World,
You are a very nice place to live on. Well at least you were a very nice place to live on. You spoilt it all when you let silly humens dig holes in you and build great buildings to block you up and let them invent spray which will eventually desroy your ozone layer and destroy the atmosphere around and kill all your plants. So persanely I think you should have more earth quakes to destroy these building but please do this on Sundays so not to kill anybody.
Your
sincerely
David

David Harris, 11

I would like it so much if men didn't have to be afraid of each other.
Anna Cygan, 16, Poland

Dear World,
I am very grateful to the world because of me having this opportunity of rectifying my feelings …
    John Wangombe, Kenya

Dear World,
Full of happiness in my heart when I hold this pen I would like to said some comment about the world…
    Steven Mututu, Kenya

…I would put right lots of other things but that would at least take a huge, big, fat volume.

Kamala Kanthan, 12

… These are only a few things which I would like to write but the lesson has just finished.
Yours sincerely
Matthew

Matthew Judge, 11

Sailen Ch Shee

Caford Health middle scool
Leoroy Road,
Pool,
Dorset

Dear world could you please cut down the price on teddey bears so that I can make my collection much better. Please counld you make less diseases so that the world counld be Happy

From Euan.

Euan Labouchardiere, 9, United Kingdom

It's a nice feeling to think about ruling over everybody.

David Smith

If I were in charge of the world no person could drink rum. If I caught anyone smoking or drinking he or she would be locked up for the rest of their lives.

Since there is so much swearing in this world I would hang anyone I found swearing, and men who fight would be jailed for the rest of their lives.

Anyone caught robbing would be stoned to death, and anyone caught blackmailing would be shot.

If I caught any men breaking canes before crop time they would be sent to jail, and the little boys would go to Summervale. If any little child was caught on the streets after nine o'clock the parents would have to give the reason.

On the first day each month, there should be a world wide prayer meeting for peace. At these prayer meeting everybody in the countries including the leaders would have to participate.

Adrian Ricardo Headley, 11, Barbados

A country should not be headed by a woman.

Humphrey Aluoch, Kenya

If I had a lot of money I would buy the world. The vandalism would be stopped by firing squad, so would burgalaries and kidnappers even murderers. Every country would be called Scotland.

All marriages would be on the same day. Every thing would be made of metal so it lasts. All food prices would go down. The only thing that could be used for transport is a push-bike. I would stop drugs and Hypothemia being sold. When going abroad you only receive one injection. Everybody would be rich.

All the seas would be called North and South. Anybody going on a boat without a ticket would be throwin into the sea.

Anybody who decided to leave the face of the earth would be electrocuted. Anybody who disobeyed me would be lashed by a whip.

Thats how I would put the world right.

Alister Ritchie, 12, Scotland

If I were more powerful than anything or anyone I would stop people exsept me useing money.

Benedict Barry, 8, United Kingdom

If I ruled the world I would have a very big palace with lots of guards and servants.

Sherry Ann Cummings, 10, Trinidad

Matthew Milner

If I ruled the world thered be generosity and kindness. If anyone was unkind (e.g. murder) or crule the penalty would be DEATH. Even if they were sorry they would still be put to death.

Toni Taylor, 12

40

Is it Hitler?

A small figure appears on the balcony of the Hotel Emperor in New York. The babble of voices stops and the people stop and look up. They see a small man with little piggy eyes set in the middle of the head, large hairy eyebrows and a small moustache. Who can it be? Is it Hitler? No, it is I Simon Wilfrid Debenham, ruler of the world. 'Hail, Debenham!' the shout rings out and shakes the ground about. 'My people. Here am I, and it is my job to make you happy. I have to put this corrupt world right. This is my plan to get rid of all crimes. The penalty for murder will be death, the penalty for rape will be death, the penalties for fratricide, matricide, patricide and sororicide will be death, the penalty for . . . .' my voice drones on and on and after five minutes of this I conclude, 'and the penalty for manslaughter will be death.' I wait for the cheering of the people but nobody cheers. The air is filled with boos and hisses and I begin to wonder whether they thought a lot of my plan or not! 'My people. All firearms are banned. From today no firearms will be made in the factories. No bullets, no pistols, no machine guns, no rifles, no bombs, the list is endless.' Hoorays erupted from the crowd and for a full five minutes I stood there waiting and listening then I pulled out my revolver and fired it into the air. The people stopped applauding and dispersed in discust realising that I could not keep my word. At last there was just one person standing in the square below and I could see that it was a small child. 'My person,' I said, 'caning and all punishments in schools will be stopped and you will have a choice of lessons. If you hate physics, chemistry, biology, maths, english, french, russian, latin, german, history and geography you may leave them out. And if you dislike the headmaster you need not go to school at all!'

'But my father is the headmaster of my school,' the child said; and without regret he pulled out one of the 'banned' firearms and fired at me. I knew no more.

S W Debenham, 13½, United Kingdom

Dalton Exley, 11, United Kingdom

Dear Prime Minister,
Crime is a bad and awful thing so if we let the cost of thing down they wouldn't have to rob would they?
Do you smoke? Well if you do I can help you stop by not leting the manufacturers make any more cigarettes.
                    Goodbye
                        From
                            Paul
                                Gibson
Paul Gibson, 9, United Kingdom

If we don't have work we must look for work. If you don't have enough money you must borrow from the bank or borrow money from your friend.
Ali-Reza Ani, Iran

Dictators would be tickled to death (because of the absence of weapons).
Andrew Dunford, 12, United Kingdom

I'd make maths easyer.
Peter Devlin, United Kingdom

Blow the world up and God can start again.
Graeme Philip Copas, 11

I try to stop striks by giving them less money.
Saskia Baguley, 9, Belgium

The only way to fix everything is to find a solution.
Joanne McLauchlan, Iran

I would put children right by hitting them. and I would stop men arguing by shouting while they are talking.
Julie Fairbrother, 8

Unemployment? There is one very good answer, get more jobs.
Belinda Sacks, 11

I would let miners retire when they like, so that they wouldn't always be on strike.
Fiona Bangert, United Kingdom

You would have to banish greed. To do this the good and bad people would need to be singled out. This could be done by having two lists marked good and bad, right from your first day at school. If you did something good (an errand or showing good manners) your name would go up on the good list. If you were bad your name would go up on the bad list and you'd sit on the bad side of the class.
Pippa Lilly, 10

All the taxes in the world I would burn them. I would give the poor people 5,000 pounds each.
Gary Sheehan, 9

if I were the ruler of the world. I wood change people from fighting. and then Ann told me. but how? I wood say please be good. and then they were good and they were never bad agin.
Sandra Williams, 7, Belgium

First I would change all the cars into horses. Then I would let all the animals out of the zoo. I would then make a machine that could stop a volcano. I would do what robin hood did, rob the rich to give to the poor. I would then stop school.
Vina Madgwick, 9, United Kingdom

The use of fire-arms would be banned, other than in the armed forces.
William Brown, 11

Instead of the animals eating one another and other human beings I would make them eat straw.
Felicia Gaskin, Barbados

I think that people should talk the same because you can't understand them. Like the Indians. They should learn English.
Donna Read, 9, United Kingdom

I would bring all the money in and share it out. When my share is gorn I will bring it back in again and share it back out.
Mark Andrews, 9, United Kingdom

if I was the ruler of the world I would change and make peace and I'd do it like this. This is how I am going to do it I would send a very important letter to the soldiers and the soldiers read it. the end
Christopher Lucarelli, 6½ Belgium

If all the poor people dressed up as nice as they could I think every one would care for them.
Chris Skinner, Iran

I would give money to robbers so that they would never rob again. I would give the World out fairly so that there would be no wars and everybody would live happily for ever.
Nicholas Page, 7, Belgium

Fishing is important as well. We haven't got many fish any where. I would catch a fish then keep it until it has babies. If it does not have any babies I will get another fish.
Christopher Stevens, 7, United Kingdom

There should be more shops so that people aren't so squashed in them.
Gerald Rix, 9, Spain

If I wher to make the world a beter place I would get a magishan and tell him to mak a spell on the volcanos all over the world so that they would turn up side down when they are going to erup

Rafiq Siddiqi, 9, United Kingdom

Politicians make promises and there are too many promises.

Julie Page, 12

If I could find a person who would be sensible to take over the Govirment I would.

David Milburn, United Kingdom

I don't see why we should have a government, MP's, Houses of Parlament or Westmister. The news readers are always telling us about the goverment and about budgets. After all cave men survived without them.

Miles Hutchinson, United Kingdom

The Chancellor of the Exchequer takes a lot and gives a little. My dad gives a lot and takes little. He is rather grumpy about it but doesn't complain.

J Carter, 12

S L Norman

I will concentrate mainly on how I would improve Britain. For a start, there would be an all women government. All the women on the government would work together as a team, which would mean the end of all our political problems. Women are a lot more sensible than men. They wouldn't bellow at one another from one side of the House of Commons to the other, nor would they screw small bits of paper up and throw them at one another. As women have to sort out their family budget, they would be able to handle the financial matters.

Natalie Markham, 13, United Kingdom

Why should we have a government, we have the Queen? We should only keep the Prime Minister if he and all the other MP's would stop arguing.

Katie Openshaw, United Kingdom

I would change every man in every goverment.

Julie Davies, 12

The Chancellor ought to be called Oliver Twist because he's always asking for more.

James Carter

Dear Politician,
When you make a speech my dad always shouts at you and swears, so I want to ask you t stop doing your AWFUL speeches!! When this man was on tele my dad kept on saying good. But when you were on tele my dad turned the tele off. Down to the point. I would like the world to stop swearing, so that means you have to stop doing speeches.
From
Roger Walsgrove
PS I am not going to vote for you.

Roger Walsgrove, 10, United Kingdom

Politicians and statemen play a great role. I would allow only such persons whose conduct, character and way of life is blotless, free from all pollution to become statesmen. Of course, those who are morally lofty and high.

Mohammad Ayaz, Pakistan

You sovereigns all over the world, keep peace and rule in justice! People in power are tempted to become proud to subdue and exploit the others instead of serving and helping them. Communistic governed countries oppress and persecute people who dare criticise and have their own way of thinking. And yet, only in freedom life becomes attractive and manifold and people are happy and creative.

Gabriele Kleindl, 17, Austria

I think that if someone is put at the top to govern then they should be proud to have that position and not use it for there own benefit, because if you have noticed taxes go up but no hospitals or roads are built, or anything like that. For, I think it is ridiculous the way any charity should have to appeal to the public for money, for poor handicapped children or some other urgent cause because this is what the government should pay for.

Fiona Lowrie, 12, United Kingdom

'Politics', what is this word which rules the Earth, the world of our dreams and desires, wonderful and unique for us? What is this word which sentences millions of people to death. There is sadness in the world of my dreams as well, because the politicians speak about peace, but at the same time they are wondering whether to start production of the neutron bomb — so 'clean' and 'humanitarian'!

Gwidon Wojcik, 17, Poland

Freedom is a gift from the sky, each individual must profit from it by avoiding giving orders.
Kafih Mohamed, 15, and Mouahid Mohamed, 15

On what I have seen, especially in the continent of Africa, most of the heads of state do not understand the word democracy because they take overturning governments as easily as drinking tea and for your information when they are doing that a lot of people die aimlessly.

Joakim Oloo, Kenya

A description of a person I think really takes from society and contributes very little? As a generalisation I would say the government fits under this heading. A few centuries ago each district used to have its squire. He was the man who took taxes and made people grind corn on his mill. At least in those days the squire gave back most of what he took by making sure that everybody was catered for. Today the government can be thought of as a type of 'gathering of squires', but squires who don't really benefit the people as a whole.

Paul Tarrago, 14

I would put the Opposition into goverment, and if they were as bad as this lot I would kick them out.

Nigel Smith

Susanna Hansen, 12, Denmark

45

Craig Hughes

Dear Your Majesty,
I do not wish to be impertinent, but I would like to suggest one or two ways in which this nation could be bettered. You ought to snatch a bit more power for yourself (don't be too greedy). Litter fines should be put up a couple of thousand pounds. Don't sack the PM just yet, he may come in handy. By the way, how would you like to travel on a filthy bus every day. I know I speak for thousands. Why can't you erayz buses? One thing you must do immediately is scrap that comprehensive education lark. It's a load of rubbish. Don't scrap the C of E. I like watching the enthronement of the Archbish. on t.v.. Talking of world problems, what about Field Marshall Amin. Not that I don't like him, but he is a nuisance. Why can't you get MI5 to kill him? Do stop those nationalisation bills, I don't really understand them. Why not scrap death duties (it's a lovely day for it).
If you carry out all these instructions Britannia should rule again. But if not try again next week.
I am your most obedient, loyal trustworthy & everloving servant,
M. Linfoot
Matthew Linfoot, 12, United Kingdom

Wages for school children — I think this is necessary to keep their interest — one pound and a bag of sweets because the little darlings do work hard. But of course you would only give it to the elevens and over.
Jackie Sperring, 12

Dear God,
I am disgusted in the way you treat Canterbury. Just last Friday the Queen (God bless her) had the courtesy to visit us and you let those girls from our other school say 'We want to see the Queen (God bless her)'. All they succeeded in doing was getting a bad name for us fellow schools in the paper. Right that is what I am disgusted about. Why do you let East Kent road-car Corporation be so stupid? you must grow a special brand of people in incubators or something. Honestly would you like to pay 23p to go two miles on a bus? And your biggest boob yet the irish, the thickest people in the world (actually they're cleaverer than our form master). Furthermore school dinners (yuk!). It is horrible (although we are grateful to have it). It's last year's left overs. And you. YOU! sitting there watching me write this letter might I suggest you supply. When I meant the irish were thick I meant those cold blooded IRA. I think sometimes you like bloodshed. Here are some answers to your problems. IRA — make a flash of lightening hit all members and help the peace movement on their way.
School dinners — you could at least make cook have a bit more imagination. Think on this you may laugh but tell me what you think of my ideas in four words.
Yours etc
Craig Hughes

Heaven
Sky
Infinity

Dear Craig,
I received your letter here are your four words
A LOAD OF CODSWOLLUP!
From God
Craig Hughes, 11, United Kingdom

Dear World,
If I were you I would do a little earthkick in Spain. But only when we had to go to school. I think every boy and girl will like it. I dount like school because the teacher is always naging. But I think she gust wants to make us learn good maners even if they are to bouring.
Sonia Bernardini, 10, Spain

I would get rid of bad people
I would get rid of bad people
And certainly get rid of people
Who write things twice

Christopher Marsh

Dear World
I would give Maggie Thatcher the sack for a start, then when I have been elected I would persuade Russia into the common market (I only hope she is not already in it) and therefore noone would dare to declare war on Britain, what with America and Russia and Britain they don't stand much chance (unless another twit of a Hitler is born). Then when I have done that I would declare war on Ireland (Southern) who (I hope) would promptly surrender, thus ending all the London bombings killings etc. And by this time the Queen *should* have died (no insult) I would then have an election as to who should be the King (or Queen) and by this time I should be quite popular (not Ford) and therefore be elected King (not Queen). I would then be in a very cushy position and once the National Front have been dealt with, I would storm into Television house (I hope there is one) and get rid of Batman, Doctor Who, 6 Million Dollar Man, and put more Frank Spencer on instead. Once this is done I would order my many servants to put more cartoons on instead of all the starting music advertisements etc. This ought to lighten everyones spirits. Bus fares would go down (I hope) and all high rise schools would have lifts. Then when people grow up they will not be vandals and hooligans. Also football should be played in a more mannerly way and thereafter (I would hope) there would be no rioting or football hooligans and as Britain has (in my world) set such a good example most countries (not all) will (I hope) follow in Britains footsteps and by now I should be getting old in age (ah) and would go out into the world and seek out a new king.

Geoffrey Knott, 11½ United Kingdom

There are lots of volcanoes erupting, you cannot stop anything like that You could not put a volcanoe back together. People who try to do that must be nuts. Some people are.

Derek Munday, 8

*Dear Goodies,
Are you really Goodies if you are here's your chance to prove it. I'm writing to ask you to put things right with the world like war, o.b.e's, ect, ect. Here's a few suggestions. You could stop war by starting a war with the people who fight in wars. And bombing in Northern Ireland you could talk about over tea and scones. Money is another problem, everybody fighting and killing for it my solution is to give it all to me. And instead of bullets make bigger gun barrels on guns so they'll fire trifles and custard pies. Good luck.
Yours sincerely,
Ian*

Ian Spicer

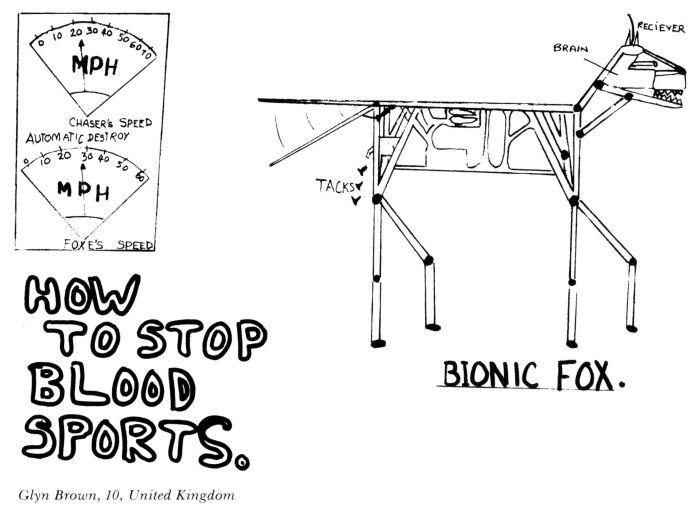

HOW TO STOP BLOOD SPORTS.

Glyn Brown, 10, United Kingdom

BIONIC FOX.

My Design for a Machine to Do Quite a lot of things

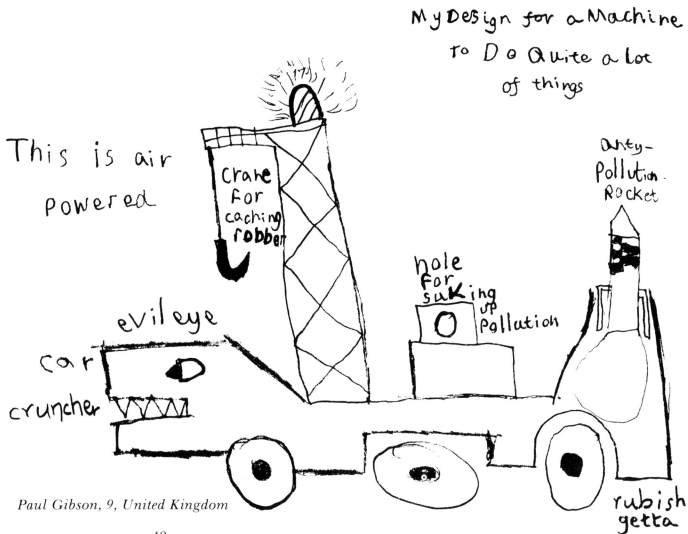

This is air powered

Crane for caching robber

hole for suKing up Pollution

Anty-Pollution Rocket

evil eye

car cruncher

rubish getta

Paul Gibson, 9, United Kingdom

48

To put the world right I've now invented a machine. Its last invention of all the world. Its name is Supervery machine. I could put there all sorts of people like babies, boys, girls, men, women, old, young, sad, happy, big, tall, fat, small, thin, etc. I could transform esqueletons to normal people. It only takes a second for each person. In that short second people change exactly good with no bad ideas and no violence. That person will born very old and die when they were babies. I like the world like that. At each birthday people will have one year less. I wouldn't like violence or sadness so I have made a plan that now when a man dies people will laugh and when he is born the people would cry.

As I said I don't like sadness but to fabric my machine I couldn't find a piece of an important motor so I had to do without it. So I had to make people sad when someone was born (as died). This machine will stop criminals and people with bad ideas. This machine will make people as they wanted to be. Big people will not know anything and young people knew everything. Everybody had to have a plan of their life. When they wanted to stop their life they could. Every one to try that machine had to pay me £1.00. I like the world like that.

Cristina Peco, 10, Spain

I would give a free holiday for everyone. I would make good people very famous indeed. I would give out factories to people who wanted them. I would let everyone go to a pantomine free. I think films that are long should be made shorter. I would make wages go up to 2,000 pounds a week. Bikes should never have a puncture. Everything should be low price. I would ban carol singing outside. I would stop flowers dying. I would have prisons pulled down. I would make a machine to do school work for children. I would make everything new and bright. I would make the year be so much longer, but I would still let there be a christmas. I would make maths easy. I would give children a baby to play with. I would make beds nice and warm. I would make mothers and fathers love the children.

Amanda Warner, 8, United Kingdom

I would make buildings vandal proof so if some one threw a stone it would bounce back and hit them on the head and give them a mighty bruise and a bump.

Raju Kapadia, 10

I would stop war by building a big ditch just big enough for the tanks to squeeze in but when there in they can't get out. I would make the planets come closer together with one metre thick cable, tie it to each planet and pull them closer together, so we could explore them. I would join all the land together. I would make a safe coal mine like a house. I would evacuate Irland and then flood it. I would make cliffs saffer. I would make fire proof matches.

David Keating, 9, Belgium

Tahirou Mahamadou, 14, Upper Volta

Cristina Peco

49

Ouygu Ayoin, 15,
Turkey

50

I could take the engines out of the car and fit pedals into it and it would stop all the smoke.

Catherine Playfoot, 9, United Kingdom

I'll deal with thoose cars. I'll put a metal cap over the cars exhaust pipe and the cap has a little hole in it there is a fan inside the exhaust pipe and when the exhaust with the carbon dioxide gos thogh the fan blows air in to the exhaust and makes the carbon dioxide misks up with the air and then the exhaust gos out of the exhaust pipe at a tremendous speed and the car gives a little or a big jerk.

George Jeffery, 9

There is a shortage of petrol soon it will be horses again. If we ran out of petrol I would dig and dig until I had got petrol unless I hit a pipe. The pipes are important to the people who made them because of the shortage of petrol I wish that I could make a pipe that oil can go through to make it go a long way down in the ground first I would dig until I reached some oil in the ground when I had got down and got the oil I would put the pipe over the oil but if the oil did not go in the pipe I would make a little hole in the pipe so it would go in the pipe that is what I would do about the shortage of oil in England. That is what I would do if I ruled the whole wide world in England.

Christopher Stevens, 7, United Kingdom

Dear Prime Minister,
Could you invent flying bikes so I can go to cricket without pedalling and making my legs ache. And I was wondering if I could go around the world painting all the trees blue, because blue is my favourite colour. Please can I have a mechanical pen because my arm aches when I write. If you really would like to go to America, please bring back a pet crocodile, because I keep on wishing that I had one. On the news tonight please can you ask someone to say that nobody really wants to be sick, and if nobody wanted to be then people must avoid spreading germs.
From
Joan Teresa Pozzoli

Joan Teresa Pozzoli, 8

I would make soft things and anything cood go over it so that there would be no aeroplane crashis I woud make it with wool and sheep skin. and if a car over ternd it woud not smash.

Owen Rowland, 7, Belgium

My Design for a Machine To pick up Litter

To pick up litter we could get a airplane and it can go across the streets and the plane can suck the litter inside the plane

GAVIN'S PLANE

Gavin, 9, United Kingdom

51

Someone should invent an extra pair of hands.

Amanda Warner, 8

If I could clean the world I would make lots of machines that would help me. It would be quite big and have lots of arms holding dusters, mops and anything you would use to clean up. The machine would not cost much because it would be made of junk from rubbish tips so it would clear up the rubbish tips and that is what I want to do. The machine would be about 7 foot high and 15 foot long. This would not get in traffic jams because I would abolish cars and go back to horses so my machine would have to have a kind of suction pipe trailing along behind because the horses would make the place dirty.

Linda Davies, 11, United Kingdom

I think that all the factories should have a chimney going into the ground. And war had not been invented. It would be better if there were no hunters. And that if litter fell on the floor it would dissolve. I wish that you did not need to go to school because you knew everything. I wish that babies could walk when they were born.

Dara Malek, Iran

I would call a dentist and make him make a plastic covering for my teeth so that you can slip them on and have sweets and no bad teeth.

Eileen McDermott, 11

I have an idea. I would join all countries by bridges so that all people could live like brothers.

Manos Tengeris, 9, Greece

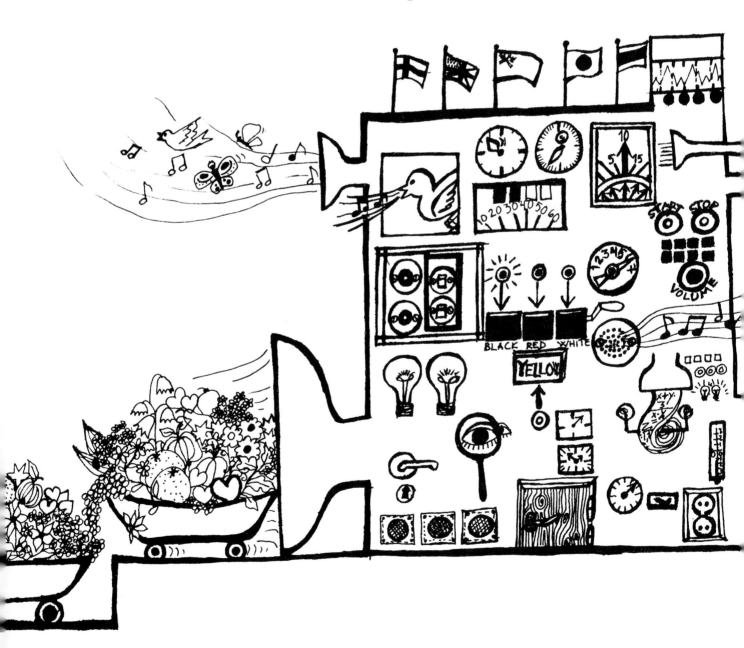

If I ruled the world I would invent a non-boredem machine to keep hooliganism down. I would invent a non-fatenning food.

Emma Spear, 9

Bombing in Ireland brings death and destruction so my solution is time bombs with flag inside which pop up and the flag shows BOOM on it. On to my next subject alcohol it brings accidents even deaths so we have to find a way to dispose of it but how? Easy — use the bottles of alcohol for army target practise a very simple solution.

John Kendrick, 11

I would make sure that their is no cliffs around, because people can fall down them.

Tracy Johnson, 11, United Kingdom

I would bring icebergs to the deserts so I would water the deserts.

Octavio Arriola, 9, Spain

Tiina Sokka, 15, Finland

I would like it if my mumy had ten pairs of hands and feet. She could clear up the house all at once. I would like to be god because I would have some magic and I could do anything in the whole whole world.

Claire Sohavenin, 7

I'd like dentists to make a drill you can't feel at all that's what I'd like the dentists to do, it would be better for children I think.

Tracey Tanner, 8

Inventors have invented lots of things, so why haven't we invented something to make us smaller or an invention what makes the world larger?

Simon Jones, United Kingdom

More, more, more

If I put the world right I would have more doctors and nurses. I would hang hi-jackes for ten years. I would make more toys. I would make more motorbikes. I would make flying saucers. I would have more detectives in the world. I would make more swimming pools. I would make more jet planes. I would make things go much faster. I would make more and more rockets. I would help old people. I would like more ships. I would like more prisons. I would kill criminals and dump them on the moon. I would make more spitfires and huakanes. Making more trains and make them more comfortable. Make more milk flotes. Make more battle ships. More car ferries. Make more racing cars. Make more houses for people to live in. I would give everyone a car to have. I would have more shops. I would have more shoes. I would have more Sarfari parks. I would have more zoos. I would have more museums. I would have more circus. I would have more fun fares. I would have more wrestling. I would have more holiday camps. I would have more sweets. I would have more bikes. I would have more felt tip pens. I would have more comics. I would have more books. I would have more pens. I would have more beds. I would have more television.

Sean Wilby, 9, United Kingdom

Sean Wilby

53

How to stop crime

Murdering can't be abolished because no-body can find out who hates whom all over the world.

Deokumar Singh, 15, Fiji

I wish I could tell everyone
  what not to do,
And stop vandalism once and for all,
But the trouble is that in this world,
I'm really rather small.

Jane Walker

I would say that gun making factorys would have to close down except they could only make guns for policemen. And policemen don't have to be serious. I have always thought policemen were but I saw some policemen eating hotdogs and laughing.

Nicola Thomas, 9

If I caught any person outside after eight o'clock I would put them in jail. Since there are so many people in the world I would have to take time in doing it.

Edwin Alleyne, 10, Barbados

Suppose there is a man near you, you have a very beautiful fountain pen in your shirt or pant pocket, suppose, he wishes to have the pen, so he nicely pinches your pen! Suppose you come to know of the theft! What will you do! You just invite him to your place, with love you call him, say, dear friend, but he trembles; he seems much frightened! He knows that you are going to punish him, you call him and ask him 'Why he stole that pen?' He hesitates to answer. What will you tell him? What should you answer? 'Dear friend don't hesitate! You have done a mistake. Have not you? Don't do like this hereafter'. We should tell him in a nice way, that shows our affection towards him; what will he do then; he will try to realise the wrong thing he has committed. He won't commit such those since afterwards. If we have love in us, we need no watchman, need no policeman to watch us.

Paul Raj, 13, India

I would get the police and they would go every where and would go in houses and look every where. and all the men that are nasty we would put them in a big boat and sail to a nother plase.

Nicholas Stockdale, 7, Belgium

Dont Fight

Rukhsana kane
Age 8

First I would have a sort of election, where the people could vote whether all the bad people went to the moon and all the good ones stayed on earth or the other way round. I would have a pannel of good people to go with them and if any bad people turned good they would tell me and I would sent a rocket to collect them. For people who smoked I would use Venus.

Liesla Eldridge, 10, United Kingdom

I do not like people throwing stones at other people's faces. Because they'll have to go to hospital and the doctor will have to put a thing over his eye. We could stop them by walking in the middle with stones. Then he will drop his stones so will we.

Lynne Isaac

I would give the good people presents and the bad people nothing. I would pray to God that the bad people chud die erlyer. The Good people chod live till 100.

Peter Nash, 7, Belgium

What shall I do about the killing? What shall I do about that then? When we catch the person, what shall we do? Hang him, kill him or make him work? I wish the police could make him work. I wish he could clean my house out every day. Or clean my shoes.

Corinne Parry, 7, United Kingdom

Because most of us do not experience the real pain of loneliness we do not understand it. We tend to have little sympathy for the child who drowns himself in alcohol or loses himself in drugs in order to get rid of the terrible pain of loneliness, emptiness and boredom that fills his life.

Ashok Kumar, 14, Fiji

I would like to put the world right by throwing all the bad people on an island, but I expect they would want to come back again.

Wendy Avis, United Kingdom

I would stop people writing on walls, by not selling aerosol paints, to no one at all, except adults of course.

Lucy Scott, United Kingdom

Patrick Bartley, 15, Jamaica

I would put the world right,
And abolish war and crime,
By putting all the villains,
In a large desert for sometime.
In there the criminals,
Would bite, kick and kill each other,
And in the middle of the Sahara desert,
Would cause the rest of the world
     no bother.

Peter Cragg, 12

For terrorists I suggest that they should, when arrested, be made to visit the hospital where their victim is being treated. They would then see the suffering, the misery that the victim goes through, and hopefully would suffer themselves.

S J Wix, 14

Criminals shouldn't be killed. I would put them all in a country where they would produce food for the old and the poor.

Justin C Munkonge, 13, Zambia

55

I would make sure that if a person hit someone they would get hit back twice as hard.
If I saw any vandals at work I would cut their skin and put salt on.

Simon Kirkup, United Kingdom

I would punish people who would not go to church. I would also punish children who would not do as they are told. If the people tell lies I would surely deal with them.
I would punish people for stealing by staking them out on some thing hot.

Caroline Norene Bullen, 11, Barbados

I would put the bombing in Ireland right. If I caught them, I would not put them in jail, because it costs £80 to put somebody in jail. I would kill them with a rifle, I wouldn't shoot them with a shotgun because it will take too slow. Before I kill them I will have to hang them up becaus if they're just shot without being hung they might run away.

Peter Ribbens, 7, United Kingdom

Then I will stop the people who shoot an old lady or a family just to get their money I will capture them I'll shoot them on the spot where they killed the father of the familey or take them to jail for their life and feed them on stale bread or just a drop of horrible milk.

George Jeffery, 9

Some children's parents don't give them proper example. They go to the pub and get drunk. That's a bad example. The children copy their example. I shall make a rule that it would not be allowed. If people are found setting a bad example then they shall be hung.

Philippa Oxford, 9, United Kingdom

Prison cells should be the most uncomfortable place in the world. What I mean is this, that jailers should not steal or commit any offence once out of jail because of the hard life in the prison. They should not bear to think of going back. The thought should send them shivering.

Anita Devi, 15, Fiji

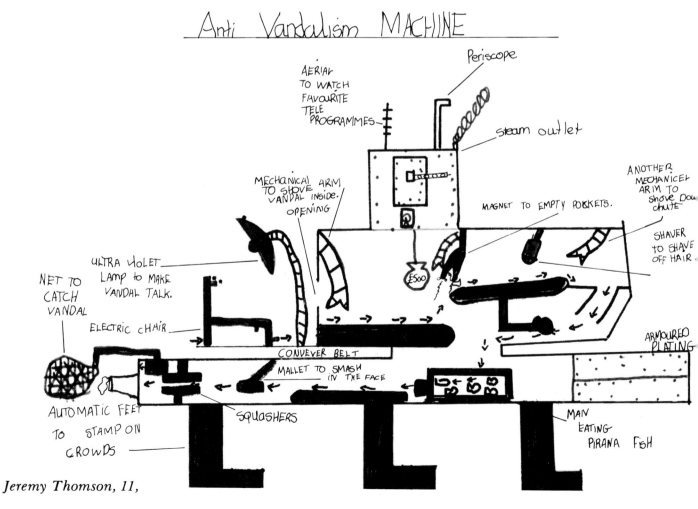

Jeremy Thomson, 11,

Crime, is the most prevalent and destructive factor of any country today. To help curb the crimes I would enforce that criminals be treated justly. First of all, for the less severe crimes, like robbery, or even stealing mangoes, this would mean the loss of a right hand. If this crime was committed twice, then the right foot would be amputated or the right ear. If the offender persisted, then the left hand, the left foot and the left ear would be severed.

Manslaughter, which is regarded as a very serious offence, would not be treated lightly. The offender would be electrocuted. For first and second degree murder, the wrongdoer would be blindfolded, tied to a tree, and shot at point blank range before a firing squad. Another solution, is that the torture of searing would be brought into play.

Treason would not be treated lightly, as the offender would be stoned to death, by being beaten with a lash or by being banished from one's country. These are very cruel ways of dealing with partakers of crime, but it must be made known that the mistake that one makes now, will surely pay dividends in the future. I also think that those who go about using indecent language should receive shock treatment or undergo rigid exercise for a day.

Lurene Gardner, 16, Jamaica

And about this Robbery, I could discuss with the members of the staff of the world about this and if any robber could be seen robbing straight he should be hanged. I could make it not to happen again.

Linus Muyagah, Kenya

If people went round killing people, I would catch them. Then I would put them in prison for their life. But if I didn't have enough money I would shoot them.

Andrew Clark, 8, United Kingdom

I would stop vandalism, by putting little children in special homes. If they were older then twenty they would be shot or hung because they should know better.

Kim Owen, 9

All lawbreakers are to be dealt with harshly in public and their punishment agonizingly.

Jannett Pusey, Jamaica

If I was the priminister I would put all the crimanals in Britain straight into jail. Then, if any more crimes were committed I would hunt them down, even if I had to do it my-self. And, if I did find them, they would really be for it!

Mark Lewis, 9, United Kingdom

Karen Keir, 11, United Kingdom

Kind little people

I will see that everyone gets a Christmas present.

Robert Moran, 8½

I would make a home to receive all the children in the street and would help them with shirts and give them trousers, shoes and whatever was necessary. I would help all the sick with drugs, medicines and many other things.

J M Clavijo, 11, Colombia
Ed: This boy is from Club Michin, in Bogota. He was abandoned as a young child.

In the shops the prices are going up. So I would try to put the prices down. I know some things have got on them 5p off or 2p off but the rest of the things need something like that on them. So that the poor people can buy food for their children.

Michele Stacey, 8

I think people in starving contries should be given much more help. Many don't have homes or a bed let alone the TV. You could put some of your pocket money in a box and send it to some charity like Oxfam. I do!

Elizabeth Knight, 11, United Kingdom

If I was to put the world right I would go round the world and see if there were any lonely people about. I would do some shopping for them if they wanted any. I would save up my pocket money to buy people food. I would buy some food for animals. If people were ill I would clean their house or feed their pets.

Sally Hodder, 8

To help the people in India we could ship water over in the swimming pools of ocean liners.

Peter, 9, Wales

If I could help the world now I would. But I have to wait till I am big because when you are big you can do what ever you want. But still I am 9 years old so I have to wait a very long time still. But in case I forget what to do I will tell you now.
First I thinking of getting some friends like Sallie, Mary, Anne, Susan and all those. They would call their friends. So we would make friends and go to Unicef or to Sanitas. Then one day we would sit together and make some plans and maps. We would be reading a newspaper when we saw a lady crying. She was crying because her baby was going to die of hunger so we would give her baby food. Then we would do a very big hospital to save people from dying. Then we would do another one in Africa and lots of other hospitals in the world. We would save many children like that. I hope you help us.

Marion Stoler, Spain

There should be more Robin Hoods, but not stealing from the rich and giving money to the poor, but stealing some time of there own and helping the poor by running errands, shopping and things like that.

Steven Goldsmith, 12, United Kingdom

We should help poor people because we wouldn't like it if we were starving. They probably havn't heard about Christmas dinners or anything.

Simone, 8 Wales

I would see that people geted plenty of food to eat or when people are ill get them their shopping or geted them drunks or get them sweet or make their beds or wash the rooms or take old people out in the fresh air or then when old people are out by themselfes and they fall down try to catch them.

Angela Harrington, 8

The cost of holidays will go down so that people can have holiday for their children and themselfs too. People will not have to pay for the holetel because some people don't have much money for all their famly and them I will keep giving them money till they can pay me back.

Jennifer Harrington, 9

if I was a ruler of the world I woud

help the poor people by giveing them

food and money and I woud get the money from

my purse and I woud give them one f each day.

And I woud get the food with my pockit mony.

Nicola Cooper, 7, Belgium

DON'T TAKE BUT GIVE.

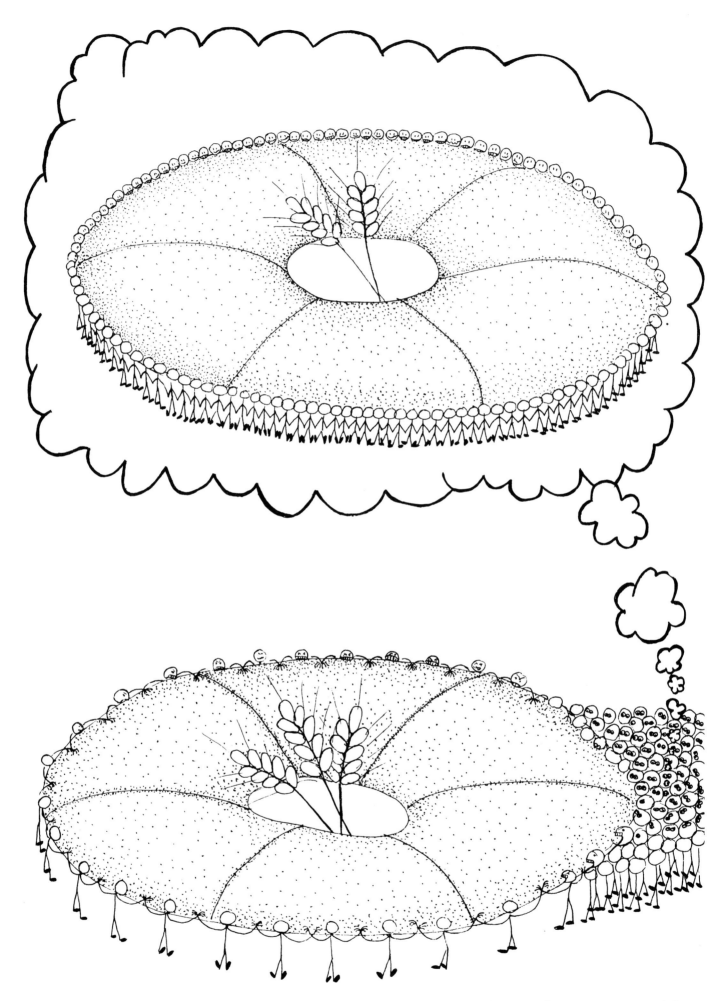

Eeva-Maria Nuorteva, 16, Finland

I cannot bear the idea of so many million dying of starvation and diseases, going without education and without the common decencies of life on account of poverty. I would much rather have equality of income — whatever the danger of such a system — than this cruel curse of poverty.

Vimla, Fiji

Only the strongest live. The strongest rule, and the weakest die. Some people wear jewlery and eat the best food, others die of hunger. They don't have money to buy food, and if they did there is no food for them to buy.

Dariush Etemad-Mogadam, 11, Iran

The world is fathomless in its evil and corruption and misplaced acts of kindness. I think that it is wrong that millionaires sit in marble halls talking in an affluent sort of way of the underpriviledged, as they throw away food for which people elsewhere are crying out. I would divide money and material things equally amongst all people and encourage people to be hospitable, generous and caring especially for older people who, in my opinion get a terrible deal.

Hamish Bowles, 13, United Kingdom

It is not only the people with power that cause trouble. It is the poor as well. They want more and more of everything. There are not many really poor people in today's civilized world because people always get what they want. If they are the greedy ones they fight for what they want and only take whilst others give. This causes bad feeling and unhappiness. People will *have* to learn to be equal, weapons will *have* to be abolished and people will *have* to give as well as take and be fair — if the world is to survive.

Colin Jewell, 13

Greed

Colin Jewell

Being hungry and poor is nothing to laugh at. It's happened to me more than once. So if there's not much money or food in the house where you live, share it. Or, if you have more than you really need, why not help out someone who hasn't enough?

Ann Ziatis, 15, Canada

If I could get rid of ambition from humanity, I could create a new world.

Merâl Doğan, 15, Turkey

Just ask yourself if the extra helping, or overexpensive foodstuff is absolutely vital to you. Stop and examine your motives for wanting. Whoever heard of needing caviare or vintage wine to be 'truly happy'?

Kathryn E M Branker, 16, Barbados

Dont be greedy

Gayle Bennett, 7, United Kingdom

61

More kind people

Rebecca Edmeades

If I ownd the world I would make sure evreone had a house. and some money. and worm clothes to wear. and I would send jokers round to make peopel laugh a lot and I would wear a smile for always. and I would give money to the poor so there would not be eney poor at all.

Mathew Titmuss, 8

if I was the ruler of the world I woud chang the fighting in to peace. and I woud make the people eat thar lunch. and I woud help the poor and make lunch for the poor. and I woud sow clothes for the poor people and I woud make muney for them.

Sian Thomas, 6½, Belgium

To the poor people I would give luxury as they have suffered enough.

Rachel Moore, 13

I would like to make things like lorrys and boats to go faster so they can go to other countrys faster to help people who are ill or have no homes.

Helen Robinson, 9, United Kingdom

I will make a little garden so that the children can go and get fruits for themselves to eat, make juice and be always contented. I will make a little park so that they can go and enjoy themselves on a Sunday after lunch and when they have done all their work.

Erma Samaroo, 11, Trinidad & Tobago

As I was having a rest under my mango tree I saw this old man with rags and no shoes. I promised myself when I grow-up I'd love to help this kind of people. I told myself when I am rich enough I would start a society called 'helping poor society'.

Rose Sanft, 12, Tonga

Dear Dilbaz,
My teacher has been telling me all about your country do you need anything like bread or biscuits or pop? I feel sad for you and your family. I will send you food.

*Your friend
Pamela, 8, United Kingdom*

Dear Dilbaz,
I have been hearing about the food shortage in your country. And I hope I can do something to help. I have seen a picture with a boy who has got the disease beri-beri. In this country we have lots of food. Would you like me to send you some butter and other things? When I first heard it I felt very sad indeed. I hope you and your people get enough money to buy the medicine and ointment you need to cure this terrible disease.

Your friend Isobel, 8, United Kingdom

Just think how lucky we are haveing a home haveing your own bedroom eating with out saving your left overs for next time. Just think how lucky we are.

Chris Skinner, Iran

I would help especially the children that are handi-capped or mentally retarded because I would like to be helped if I was like they are.

Maureen Rizzo, 11, Australia

Voltan Cambell, 12, Jamaica

If I was Queen and could rule all the world I would send food to people who needed it. I would send for blankets and food to be sent to where there had been an earthquake and volcanoes erupting. I'd love to stop people pulluting rivers. I wish I could make all the animals friendly. Like lions and tigers. I wish people would stop killing animals. I also would like to plant more trees and make more countryside. Then animals could live in peace. I wish I could stop people getting hurt when aeroplanes crash. I would invent unbreakable glass. I would like to make children quiet so that people could concentrate. I would give people houses if they had nowhere to live. Perhaps I could put bunk beds in classrooms so if it snowed people could stay in the warm. I would invent special spaceships and non-crashable aeroplanes. I would like to invent different medicines, all sorts of things. I wish people would be kinder to other people. Then everybody could be friends. I would like people to be happy. Insted of these factories I would like factories to make more money. Then poor people could become richer. I wish all people cared for animals. If they found injured animals they would take them into their houses. I would like to stand in front of people to stop them fighting. I wish people would not keep hens ore any other animals in cages too small for them. Please could people not make things dangerous. Bikes are dangerous. I would like people to love their children. I wish they would not beat children or leave them standing alone in the streets. I wish all countries had kings and queens. Then perhaps people would like the world better and stop killing other people. I wish I could make everything in this world better. I would like it if everybody could speak the language of every country. I would like to go round giving free drinks. I would like it if trips on aeroplanes didn't cost so much. It would be nice. In my world I would make children write propably and do long stories. Then teachers will not have to get angry and shout. In my world everybody would be happy everybody could go on holiday.

Rebecca Edmeades, 8,
United Kingdom

Dear Person in India
I am sorry to hear that yove had a Volcano blown up.

Love
David, 5½, United Kingdom

I would try to make the world a happyer place. By telling jokes to everybody.

Patricia Helen Lamb, 8

If I was very powerful I would buy lots of food and take it out the ethiopia and feed all the people who arn't as lucky as us in Great Britain. We are some of the luckiest people in the world.

Wendie Hobbs, 9, United Kingdom

I wish old people would have enough strength to handle cooking and things like that. And that the old men can keep there houses tidy for when people come and visit them. And I hope they get better from illneses and flues and things like that. Lots of people I hope will look after the old. And keep them warm.

Diane Barnett, 9½

I would make sure that all the children would have parents to look after them to love them and care for them. That is how I would like the world to be — love, happiness and honour thee.

Jacqueline Coyle, 11

If there are tramps I will find homes for them so that they don't have to stay out in the cold all night and day. They will wear all nice clothes and they will have lots of food and drink. They will have maids and gentlemen.

Jennifer Harrington, 9

Dear World
I would like to change the world into a happy world for the old and lonely. So all the old and lonely get visit every day. I wish the world to be a better place for my sister and me and my parents and my budgerigar and every body in the world.

Sara Feldbacher, 8, United Kingdom

You need money for buying food, but not for watching a sunset.

Andre Revesz

Money is like greed.
Listen and take heed.
The more you want the more you need.
Nothing can be worse than greed.

Stephen Wiskin, 10

Money would be thrown into one massive fiery furnace, glowing with anger, so that people can exchange goods.
Money has never, according to me, done too well because people want and need more of it each day and year. People are greedy and selfish and if they don't get what they want they go on strike, acting like children.

Sharon Randall, 13

Thousands of people are thronged in huge buildings which look like silos. Many of them withdraw and live like lonely islands. They are only anxious to enlarge their own capital. Many people think: I and maybe my family interests me, but nobody else.

Gabriele Kleindl, 17, Austria

I wish there was no money,
In this big world of ours,
No body would steal things,
Not even a small vase,
We'd all be very happy,
And learn to love and share,
To see the things that nature brings,
With time to look and care.

Laura Sloman, 11

The way to put the world to rights is to make people happy and contented. Government measures and politics do not really come into this question. Some cynics would say that the only way to do this is to distribute money, but I do not agree. For what is money? Nothing but a slip of paper. What is gold? Nothing but a metal elevated to dizzy heights because it is 'pretty to look at'.
What is life? Nothing if one does not make full use of it. So then, the goal in life is to be happy. Money and wealth is merely a means to an end, not an end.

Happiness comes to different people in varied ways. Some enjoy the 'high life', others enjoy the simple life of the countryside. This is only taste for different life-styles. However, most people like to have friends. Humans like being together.
Friendships are an important part of life. So this is really what the world needs. The key words are Friendship, Unity and Neighbourliness. That equals Fun which is the result.

Simon Robson, 14, United Kingdom

People are 'ignorant and blind' as Thornton Wilder says. They spend all their lives searching for happiness and save no time to enjoy it. They lose their happiness in searching for it. A person could spend his entire life making money, thinking that it would make him happy. Some people lose their principles and morals in search for concrete things and this is the worst that can ever happen. Some people sell their souls and lose their honour because they care so much about materialistic things!

Bahiga Abed, 16, Egypt

I dream of a world with no possessions at all. Nothing will belong to anybody except their own thoughts and possibly another person's heart.

John Manan, 15, USA

The thing to do is to crush the clocks, melt the coins and then make life and love synonyms.
'What is this life, if full of care, we have not time to stand and stare.' Don't you think that this just fits us? Yes, it at least fits me.
Today, we have become slaves of time. Life just competes between two poles, time and money. All are so busy that they can't even meet their dearest ones. Life has become flat and uninteresting. There is no spiritual happiness, no peace of mind.
When I was a small boy I had heard people saying that life is a race. I found out that yesterday it was a race to achieve love and happiness while today it is a race to achieve money and power.
Money has become a magnet and man, an iron piece. Don't you think so? We are entangled in this web of time and money. Let's fuse to break it.

Sanjiv M Mehta, 15, India

The more you get rich the more you become rivals. When you look for hatred among the poor Bushman of Botswana you can't find it. They are peaceful people.

Buzzord Goaletson, Botswana

I would encourage people to grow their own food, swapping the surplus for other materials like furniture made by someone who owns forest land, or wine made by people with vineyards, and so on.
This swapping would make money slightly less important, and would help quell the natural greed for money.

J Henthorne, 14

There is greed in small places, big places and in all types of places. The main source is 'Money'. Money causes crime and jealousy. Money causes selfishness. People are never content, they want more and more. They will never share. We human beings are the most unsatisfied creatures.

Seema Jamnadas, 14, Fiji

I imagine that the world would be much better if money stopped to rule the relations of people.

Maro Zervoudaki, 9, Greece

The generous person is the one who is willing to give up his time. Time is the most precious thing given to man. Money has nothing to do with generosity. A generous person is like a flower — it takes little from the soil but it gives beauty and air to the world.

M Philpott

Prosperity continues in this world but are we really happy? Have you ever wondered why today's high standard of living hasn't produced more real happiness; and why it hasn't lessened crime? Material wealth is not the source of happiness. A person can be happy whether rich or poor. America leads the world in crime and also in divorce. Increased wealth and prosperity should bring more happiness but it is the opposite in reality.

Anita Devi, 15, Fiji

Gold

I have eurything

Lynne Fordham, 7

Dear man,
Why do you turn your head, when I
    look at you with a question in
    my eyes?
Why do you close your eyes when
    you see my tears?
Why do you quickly withdraw your
    hands, when mine are looking for
    your support?
Why? Could it be that you are afraid
    . . . of yourself.
            Anita VrueGdenhik, 17, Netherlands

Another cross-word puzzle, maybe
_____

And children, running round
    in unseen clothes,
With swollen bellies, glaring eyes,
    wild eyes, sad eyes.
Questioning the world in which
    they have no chance to survive,
They look, and find that terrible word
    breeding all around them
...Starvation.

A word destroying all souls, all hopes,
But no! All love and life.

For when was it that he,
Yes, he, the cripple huddled
    over there in rags —
A begging bowl, a wrinkled face.
When did he last feel that
    after-dinner burden
Of a well-fed man?

And how? enquired the inconsiderate
    man,
And how are we supposed to solve
    this one?
Like sorting out a crossword puzzle.
Supplies they need — food, nurses
    maybe?
And sips his wine,
    with fat, clumsy fingers all asprawl,
And laughs light-heartedly —
            Karen Marchant, 14, Iran

In my opinion, hunger and poverty is a
disease spread by rich people who have
many more things than they need.
Some people are worth millions and
millions of money. These are the
peoples who brought corruption and
endless inflation. In our country you
can find a person is an MP or a civil
servant with salary not less than four
thousands per month. The same
person will own many hectres of rich
soil, fleets of buses, and 'fun enough'.

May God blast his soul
It would be so easy just to introduce a
rule saying that: *Nobody is allowed to
have more than two types of work.* And
that would be that. If you are a clerk you
don't trade in a provision store. If you
are an MP you don't have fleet of
'matatus'. Within about five years I am
damn sure that nearly everybody now
have work to do and something to eat.
Not like nowadays you find some
people have put nothing in their
mouth while dustbins and refusals
ditches are filled with unwanted food
from wealthy men ... many have not
even found stale bread which they can
put in their stomachs and now the rich
are dumping fresh food in bins.
Now, about invironment: This too fox
me. You find too that the so-called rich
men have big houses with many rooms.
In the other hand you find thousands
and thousands of people who live in
one-roomed cubicles. That one-roomed
cube is supposed to hold a family of five
to nine members. Imagine father,
mother, and kids snoring in one room.
The sacks which once contained pasho
makes their mattress. When the time
comes for breakfast, gruel without
sugar or sometimes nothing. The kids
develop sagging stomachs due to lack
of nutritious food. Do you know what
is happening at this moment? The rich
man is on his table surrounded by his
healthy family. The table is overloaded
with trays, plates, cups and many types
of fruit.
The streets are jammed with job
seekers. They have been told that with
education they have the world in their
pockets.
No money, no house to live in and what
have you. Oh Jesus, this world.
I am sure that not even one of these rich
men would like my idea of splitting
some of his money to those who are in
need. Damn them! I could tell them to
drop dead if they would not accept
what I have for them. You know if you
want to make yourself understood by
people you don't have to be kind to
them always. You must get tough with
them. If you kneel in front of them and
say 'please part with some so we can
give to the poor' they will just stare at
you like a creature from Mars. The best
way is to face them with a politician
face. Believe me, they would tell you
that you are a mental case and in
addition to that, you can drop dead ...
God, why do you give them all this.
            Mark Philip Musyoki, 13, Kenya

The greatest difficulty with the world at present is not its inability to produce but its unwillingness to share.

Opal Bernard, 16, Jamaica

I was sitting under my guava tree watching, thinking. Just then a huge concord jet whizzed by, I just sat there thinking, 'If I could put the world right', I thought. I'd kick out all destruction like earthquakes, war, murders, big polluting factories and even that concord that just went by. For about ten seconds I was paralysed because I was thinking so hard. If I was the king of the world I'd go right over to a place like Russia or communist China and say 'Give to poor places like India where there are many so poor that they are trying to eat the things out of a rubbish can, so poor that they have to rob to stay alive!'

But I guess they'd just sit down and let their greedy cheeks roll and just laugh all day non-stop! 'Why laugh', I would say, 'Why laugh when you should help these people who die before your very eyes and you just sit there ordering your poor servants and slaves to get you a drink, make your bed and wash your clothes. Have pity on all the poor who are desperately struggling to stay alive, do you hear? Help! Have pity!' I would yell, but that probably would make them laugh more until their fat stomachs exploded, but that probably wouldn't stop them laughing! Then I would go over to a place like England or America and ask the same of them. If they refused I would almost get on my knees and beg them 'Give $100m or £100m for the poor'.

Then my mind clicked off the rich and went to the poor at feasts and parties eating and drinking as much as they liked. Then my imagination stopped and I woke up. 'I wish it were true but it isn't'.

John Snell, 10, Tonga

Gertrudis Yolanda Andino, 12, Honduras

The fat and the thin

His face is burnt, his eyes are red,
His lips don't have any colour,
He saw the sun,
He saw the sand,
He saw his hungry mother.
What could he do?
What could he say?
He left this world for heaven.
They just can't live this way for ever.
Don't let them starve,
Don't let them die,
Please make their life better.

Atanasiu Lucia, Romania

**Much too weak
To stand up and walk.
Flies everywhere,
On their noses,
On their lips,
In their eyes,
Swelling stomachs, full of air,
Waiting to die**

FOOD

Four letters which can mean a life.

Neal, 11, United Kingdom

Look at me!
I'm a skeleton.
So feed me
And take care of me.
Give me food
And medicine.
Take me in,
Please!

Adrian, 11, Wales

To You, Man

Man
You, the genius of science
    and technology
You who claim to be Master of creation
You, selfish, curious, striving upwards
Why do you flee to your affluence?
Why do you waste money on
    unnecessary things
But insist
That you can't afford to help?
Why do you lead us to destruction?

Stop, open your eyes and see
Don't you notice the rest of us
Who are not so strong as you?
Us who cry in wars
Us who starve and live in want

Have you forgotten love?
Love which enables us to live
Love which makes all of us
Trust in a better tomorrow
Love which creates unrest in your heart
Even if it is stifled

Man
Leave your shell and come to us
Come and see our agony
Which you have brought about
Come and help!

Christine Routamo, 17, Finland

In India sometimes people do not eat
for days. The children die in their
mothers laps. You can even count the
bones in the child through the skin.
Think of the mothers whose children
just die in front of their eyes. Well
something must be done to get rid of
starvation.

Chandra Kumar, 16, Fiji

Tuula Ahonen, 17, Finland

Lots of rich people would tell me to 'get out', if I asked them to help the poor. Lots of people are too well fed and they throw lots of food away without even knowing about starving people. Some people die of eating to much in places like USA, NZ, UK, Australia.

Tavake Afeaki, 10, Tonga

Dear President Carter and Cabinet,
It appears to me that if one lives in either Africa or Latin America one's chances of having a proper, nutritious meal during one's lifetime are practically non-existent. And, to my disgust, I have also discovered that in 'first world' countries people are permitted to literally throw food away, and farmers are often paid to dump it. And I'm sorry, President Carter, but Americans are the worst offenders.
Is your distinguished cabinet *really* so heartless, so callous as to allot large sums of money for the manufacture of more deadly weapons — 'defence spending' in the face of the world's great need of food? I am appealing to government ministers in your wealthy country to facilitate the transfer of excess food. The rich world could go on a 'Save-the-Food' drive. Your people would be much healthier, I am sure. Please consider this suggestion — the future of our world depends on it.
Yours sincerely,
Maureen C Spencer (Miss)

Maureen C Spencer, 16, Barbados

As many as four hundred million people may be in peril of starving this year in Asia, Africa and Latin America. The primary factor responsible for the world food crisis is the population explosion. Population is now increasing at the rate of 80 million a year. The human race did not reach its first one thousand million people until A.D. 1830. Only one hundred years later in 1930 the second one thousand million was reached, thirty years later in 1960, the third; and it took only fifteen years for mankind to add the fourth.
Imbalance also plays an important role. There is inequality in the pattern of food production and utilization. As societies become wealthier, their consumption of animal products increases. This means that a greater proportion of basic foodstuffs such as grains and soya beans — that could feed human beings directly —are instead being converted into feed for poultry and large farm animals.
Only 16 per cent of calories fed to chickens are recovered by us when we eat the chickens. This conversion rate goes down to five to seven per cent in cattle that are fed corn to add fat and protein to their flesh before slaughter. Yet the rate at which meat consumption has increased in the rich nations has been nothing short of spectacular. The rate of increase in meat consumption has even been greater in several European nations, and in the Soviet Union, than in the United States. The net effect is that rich nations, capitalist or communist, use far more food per person than developing countries. In poor countries, such as mainland China, the average person feeds himself with some one hundred and ninety five kilos of grain each year. In the United States the average person uses more than six hundred and sixty five kilos, more than eighty per cent as animal feed.

Rajesh Kumar Patel, 15, Fiji

Tuula Kilpinen, 17, Finland

Jennifer Vetterli, 10, Canada

STOP RACISM!

The older generation did not let their children marry into other races until recently. Why were they so blind, I do not know. All they had to do was look out of the window and see kids playing. Kids of different colour, hair, strength and race, playing together as one. Copying the kids they could have stopped this growing barrier between races. Even now it is not too late and I sincerely hope my generation is more understanding. There is nothing we can do to prevent this racial disharmony until each and everyone of the older generation dies who have hatred in their hearts for different races.

Anita Devi, 15, Fiji

Tribalism hinders some parts of the world. Jealousy arises and you find that one race separates from another. You find that if you go to his or her office to ask for a job the answer is that there is no work. The next day you hear that someone has been employed. This means that the job has been given to a relative or a person of the same tribe. Therefore I appeal that such a thing should be avoided.

Oscar Ochieng, Kenya

What I would like to be changed is to abolish all divisions between mankind, the division between whites and coloured, between rich and poor, between the different nationalities and between the different religions.

All these divisions go back as far as recorded human history. To change any of them human nature must be changed.

Claire Elek, 11, Australia

Roberto Montiel, 11, Honduras

Earth you were beautiful in olden times. You were happy, not disturbed by anything.

You were every colour: red, yellow, white, black.

Then came a tiny creature which you didn't think could bring evil to you. You were kind to it. You fed it, and it grew bigger and bigger.

To your surprise, it stood up on two legs and showed its behaviour. It tore your beautiful dress.

It started rebelling against you. Earth you have turned into something which is terrible. You have changed into something which was unknown. Gunsmoke is ruling you. There is one party, which is violence and discrimination about people's colour and rights, bloodshed to brothers and sisters, father and mother. The streams are flowing with human blood. Two people are created. One thinks he is better than the other A white man, a master, and a black man, a servant.

Vincent Kenosi, 14, Botswana

What does it matter if the colour of my skin is white, yellow, black or green, as long as my heart is as white and spotless as snow?

Laila Risgallah, 19, Egypt

A world in which all people can live, black or white. A place where all people have the same rights, a place where there is no need to lock your door and no such word as hate.

Where is this place? I want to go there.

Bill Say, 11, Australia

By the time we kids have grown up, I hope that the term racial discrimination will have disappeared. The fact that generations of the black race have led their lives with pride in their race despite all kinds of hardships is really superb. All races have their own self-pride and that is wonderful. If we understand each other's self-pride, then these sad problems would disappear, wouldn't they?

Mihoko Sugiura, 11, Japan

Have you ever thought about racism? Racism is something that is not so nice. It is when someone makes fun of you if you're a different colour or if your eyes are different. I never really thought of it until today. Now let me tell you a little story. I tell when I was only three years old mom and dad decided to go to Canada. My sister and I thought it was going to be fun. Naturally we went to the nearest school. I walked into the classroom. It was frightening for me. Everyone stared. The next day everyone started to call me names. I was deeply hurt. It took me a few years to ajust but today I am doing just fine. So the next time you got to call somebody names because they are different from everyone else, think about my story. I know that person will appreciate it.
Mary Hong, 10, Canada

Marsha Mungal, 9, Canada

71

Let me be what I am

Zeba Rehman
Age 7

The world is a beautiful place, but this beauty cannot be displayed in all its grandeur if it is shielded by sham, drudgery and broken dreams.

There is one, and only one main aim, that I would endeavour to attain if I were to put the world right. That aim would be to let mankind be more aware of one another, and in so doing, man would realize that his brother has his own labours and aspirations and each is working to attain his aim in life.

Jo-Ann Miller, 16, Jamaica

Most violence is caused by our being too big-headed to give way to another cause and because we let our hatred get the better of us. Surely we hate our people to allow them to butcher each other and people even get medals for this. I cannot imagine what the world would be like if we all loved each other but if we learn to bear and even appreciate each others customs or beliefs and forget the long born grudges we will be much happier.

Nickolove Lovemore, 13, Barbados

I have a right
To choose my own beliefs
Without having somebody
Laugh at me
Just because I don't
Believe in what
You believe in, I am not mad!
But using my rights.

If I want to dress up
Like an African
That is my business
Not yours,
So leave me alone
And don't ridicule me
On sight
After all it is my right.

When you see me
Join women's lib.
Don't tell me I am trying to
     be a man
Leave me alone
Stop trying to change me
I am an individual
Let me be what I am,
It is a free country after all,
So let me have my rights!

Cheryl Brathwaite, 17, Barbados

Can we change the world? No! but we can see to it that the next generation will have the instruments to do it. We can build more international schools and camps so children of one country would live with children from other countries and learn their customs, their problems and the fact that, after all, we are all the same. This situation would force us to have an international language (Esperanto?) that would make people understand each other better.

Eldit Beiles, Israel

Every one has the right to live, so live and let others live.

Karoon Wata, 12, Fiji

We must give the same truth to the women and men. If we did so, we would put the world right.

Adviye Denizer, 14, Turkey

If I ruled the world I would order two big black pots and in one I would put the people and make them all one colour. In the other pot I would put all the religions and make the people all the same religion.

Amber Macdonald, 11, United Kingdom

Just because someone doesn't believe in your God, that's no reason to kick him in the teeth and keep on doing it! His skin may be a different colour from yours ~ so what! Wrapping paper comes in all different colours.

Lynn Govan, 15, Iran

Why so much injustice? Why so much division in a world of today where the meaning of brotherhood is totally rejected.
The word brother will not make sense again until we accept that we must put ourselves in another's skin, to understand him, and to treat him as we wish he'd treat us.

Marie Claire Jean, 16, Haiti

Not understanding each other is the most thing which is destroying peace. We should know every language because if you hear other people talking in English you think that they are scolding you.

Farasten Kadgunge, Rhodesia

Every man is our relative, so love should be established in men. We should not show any indecent manner in our saying or walking that may hurt anybody or that may hinder the establishment of love.

Farid Patel, India

If you want others to respect you, then learn to respect them.

Karoon Wata, 12, Fiji

Cheryl Braithwaite

Respect each other's National Flag and learn as many languages as possible to get to know each other.

Fathima Rahiman, 10, India

Esra Asula Arin, 13, Turkey

Animals' Lib

Animals are just as important as man, and should live. The world was given to man and animal not just man.

Karen Shaw, 12

If I ruled the world I would stop people keeping wild animals I would stop bull fighting and fox hunting stop lions in circuses ide make a law about that if any body brock that law I would send a police man to ask why you did it.

Christine Adaway, 7

Chickens give eggs for us to eat and all we do is feed them. I think this is real generosity and nobody ever thanks them. The same goes for other animals who are killed without being thanked!

N Gibson, 12

I would like to stop destroying animals and their homes. How would we like it if giants came and destroyed our homes and killed us.

Sunil Maini

We should stop killing animals,
They might rise in revolt,
Great big Gorillas holding
　machine guns,
Robbing a bank.

Aneil Bedi, United Kingdom

Blood sport has become a costom in England and some people would not like to see it go. But I think it should be stopped, or how would you like to be chased by foxes and rabbits, you would not like it would you?
I think there should be a law against blood sports. I would put people in prison for thirty years. Then I would make remote control animals instead of real ones and the huntsmen could chase that if they wanted to.

Mark Perrin, 10, United Kingdom

Let old birds have old birds homes.

Emma Simpson, United Kingdom

I am a silver fish swimming
　in the stream
Last night I had such a horrible dream
I dremt I was laying on a silver dish
But mummy quickly came along and
　said
'Wake up fish'.

Helen, 10

I would abolish the cock fighting that some countries still have. I think it is cruel and unfair to the hens.

Nicholas Wright, 13

I would abolish the killing
　of creatures.
Zoologists open them up,
　to look at their features.
Animals in zoos are laughed at and fed.
'They should be in the forest,
　Yes that's what I said.'
What wild can they go to,
　if it is all gone.
Think of your house,
　all lined with foam.
It's probably standing
　on some animal's home.
Think of your beautiful
　Christmas day dinner.
The luckiest of two chickens,
　is the one that's the thinner.
At Christmas you sing and you dance.
Think of that chicken,
　who didn't stand a chance.

Andrew Crabb, 12, United Kingdom

I would stop bull fighting because a man could be killed and we don't know if the bull want's to die.

Lynda coke
Age 8

Great Britain

Michael van Luven, 8, Canada

74

The whale, powerful graceful,
yet useless on land.
Slaughtered for its blubber,
oils and other luxuries.
Please god let us kept the whale,
powerful graceful.

Johan de Vries, 12

How would you like
To balance a ball
And not let it fall

How would you like
To stand on a table
When you're not really able

How would you like
To jump through a hoop
With flickers of fire
Afraid of the wire

Some live in the jungle
Some live in the sea
We are proud creatures
Please let us be free

Clare Lee Warner, United Kingdom

How would you fill to be one day happy with joy and the next day killed and someone ateing you for supper?

Chris Skinner, Iran

We read the human race is the highest
form of animal, but what rights does
this give us to make plaything, games
and slaves of other animals. Animals
are ment for us to love, to care for, to
help, not to use in an exihibition, like a
piece of china.

Fiona McGuinness, 12

Anand, 13, India

The beautiful earth

Dear World,
I have been a part of you and I appreciate you a lot. You contain so many beautiful and lovely things. I feel locked-up in rapture when I think of you. Such plants, the many coloured trees and sweet-smelling flowers; the sea, which is sometimes calm and tranquil and at other times rough and angry. These all help to make you so interesting.
The people who make you up and who dwell within you can be so lovely, gentle and kind-hearted. When I think of the members of the Salvation Army, the missionaries, all the members of voluntary organizations dedicated to helping other people, I realize just how lucky I am to be a part of you, World! The Heavens declare your loveliness and it is a comfort to me just to look at the stars or feel the rays of the sun on my body.
World, don't ever change. There is nothing wrong with you. It is only the hearts of men which need rejuvenating and a new purpose.

I love you, World
Yours faithfully,
Jean West, 16, Jamaica

Would you like to live in another world
Like in Mars, Venus or the Moon;
If there's the promise of paradise
And joy all year round?

I want to stay here,
The place of my birth and my strivings;
I welcome whatever obstacle may
  come,
The earth is my own, truly mine!
Francisco o Acosta, 12, Philippines

Nature is beautiful

A Teleca, 10, Trinidad

The Earth

The earth is round, with the land brown, the night is dark, and the day is light, the leaves are green, the sky is blue, the trees are green, the seas and oceans are blue, the rivers are blue, the Earth is good.

Jose Ocariz, 9, Spain

We all complain about air pollution. But we talk so much about it, that we forget that there are good things besides air pollution. Let scientists 'break their heads' about the problem, and you can look at the lovely views, smell the flowers and enjoy your life — because there are many lovely things in the world, and its a pity to waste them. Just be happy, enjoy your life, and try never to get angry. Always smile and you will see how lovely and good the world will be.

Anat Blum, Israel

I Love The world because It's so beautiful.
The People are beautiful.
The things in the world are beautiful.

Betty Ann Cumberbatch, 10, Trinidad

77

The yellow sun shines on the yellow daffodils and the yellow crocuses which bloom in the meadow. Yellow is the bright happy colour of spring.

Andrew, 10, United Kingdom

Oh! Khalahadi you are not
Important and you are poor
But your people live peacefully
Makers of happiness all the time.
The mother of great Elands
My eyes are on you
Bushmen are in your hands
You are my mother's land.
I'm proud of you, my mother's land
My eyes are on you
Khalahadi land of great lions.

Lopang U Modisakgomo, 16, Botswana

How beautiful is Botswana
Country of blacks
Country of animals like springbok
    and lions
Country of people who eat food
    which they plough for themselves.

How beautiful is the country
A country of happy people
Country of people who dance
    tswana songs without any war
Country of wild animals and
    tame animals.

How good are the people of Botswana
People who eat sorghum and
    meat of animals
Country of milk which flows
    like water
Country of cows which are milked,
    being asleep
Country of men who are always
    busy ploughing
And doing some difficult work.

How good are the people of Botswana
People who help the blind, cripples
    and those who are poor
People who work for themselves
    until they are blind.
Oh my heart is always in Botswana
Where I was born by my parents
Country of long trees and
    beautiful grass
Country with rain and water
    flowing in streams.
Long live Botswana.

Boitumelo Kgopiso, 16, Botswana

What is the nicest thing that has happened to you?

The nicest things that have happened to me are when I go into the woods and fields and I can run about and feel free, and when I go out and play with my friends horses.

Jayne, 11

Was when the nurse told me that my grampa was going to live after a stroke.

Catherine, 10

Was when I fell and hurt my head in a street and a friend came and helped me.

Colin, 11

Is when my brother goes into a coma he doesn't die from.

Karen, 11

78

Tayfun Yagdereli, 15, Turkey

1. The world is beautiful.
2. I love the world.
3. I love every body.
4. The children in my class are beautiful
5. When children are at play they have plenty fun.
6. Children are nice.
7. Children have fun every day.
8. We like to play at schod.
9. The game is nice.
10. We like the world.

Maureen Salvary, 7, Trinidad

In the world there are over one bileon animals, they are killing kangroos by the mileon I want to stop this someday. If not I will set up a canpain. This is going to be hard but it will hapan. The Elephent's are still being killd for ther task there alredy is a canpain but ther need's to be a biger one. This is inportent the all animel's get protection. If not there be dying. This is what canpaining's all about I have done my conservationet badg at cub's.

Stephen Wilkins, United Kingdom

I think it would be better if there were no cars and no planes, because it makes the air bad and people get weaker and weaker because they don't go out for walks.

If there was no smoke the air would be much better and cleaner. If there was no dirty water the fish would not die and the people would not get sick. If we shared the oil we would have no wars. Someone should tell everyone.

Kamisaka Isao, 11

S Strike

80

Hunting would definitely be stopped,
I think it is cruel to destroy animals.
Chickens, lambs and pigs will
    unfortunately have to be killed.
After all, we can't all become
    vegetarians,
Especially not me,
I couldn't be,
I love chickens too much.
Melissa Jeanne Rizzi, 10, United Kingdom

I would make all the Yoboes clear up the streets and ban parking and knock down the citys so that there would be no more accidents with cars and replace them with fields of grass. But I would leave London as it is because of people who do not like the country side.

    Petula Easton, 10, United Kingdom

If there is a shortage of water I would tell people to pull there chain at the end of the day instead of every five minits. Because every time you go and pull the chain it uses a gallon of water gone. But in the whole world about 10 millon. Or even more water.

    Diana Lynch, 9, United Kingdom

My ambition is to become a footballer or to study Nature. If I was a conservation expert I would give birds full protection, and study them — meney peapol shode know the dodo is extinct I whont to brerd animal's some day. And try to bread the brids that are extinct.

    Stephen Wilkins

GIVE A HOOT DON'T POLLUTE

Joe Iozzo, 10, Canada

I would try to make the world be like New Zealand because if you drop a bit of paper you pay a fine of fifteen pounds.

    Andrew Clark, 9

If I were in charge of the world I will stop people from chopping the trees down because trees have feelings to.

    Robert Moran, 8½, United Kingdom

Hi, my name is Anna. Have you thought about pollution? Well I have, and when I did it sounded stinky!

Anna Colangelo, 10, Canada

Where are the flowers?

Oh World you are so beautiful
Thy hills, thy wide grey sky,
Thy mists that roll and rise.
The trees so slenderly built,
The deep blue seas and Ocean
Oh World you are beautiful.

They have tried OhWorld
To destroy you,
To destroy your beautiful sceneries.
The factories which pollute the air,
With smoke and dust,
They try Oh World to destroy you.

They can't destroy you Oh World
Because each and every morning
You are new,
The air smells so fresh and lovely.
The hills look greener, the skys greyer.
Oh world you are beautiful,
Please stay that way.

Kathleen Williams, 14, Jamaica

My children should have a safe world. I fear most of all the dangerous side of technology such as pollution of air and water. I don't know how my children will breathe. I sometimes watch these awful fumes that escape from cars, buses and many other machines. I sit there breathing and knowing that these poisons entering my body may affect my health. Still, I breathe. What can I ever do about it? I wish my children could feel safer and breathe with ease.

Sami Raghda, 15, Egypt

No-one cares for the
  fresh green grass,
That whimpers in the cool crisp air,
Getting trampled by feet that pass,
Am I the only one to care.
Quivering poppies dance around
Prop up their weary stems
The muddy stream trickling down
No longer like a gem
But tin cans littered here and there
Rattling an untuneful song.

Sonia Saxena, 10

Many new inventions were made and the most fatal of them were poisons. Factory chimneys poured them forth and trees died. Birds were left without nests and the little insects which lived under the bark were poisoned. Little birds ate them, bigger animals, in their turn, ate the little birds. The poison spread. It penetrated everywhere, into the air, into the water, into the earth. Many animals could not find food or shelter. Even people ate poison in their food. Man and his inventions messed up everything. It is man's job to clear up his mess, for he cannot live without nature. Nature is the beginning of everything and man is part of it.

Maria Tromp, 14, Finland

Juha Espo, 16, Finland

The world was once
  a beautiful place
But now it stands a monument
  of disgrace.
Fear everywhere, crime in the air
And sorrow yet to come.
Mother nature looked with
  pitiful eyes
And then began to realize,
That trees, meadows and hills,
And beautiful daffodils
Would be the solution to
  man's problem.
But man began to destroy nature
And one day nature repelled
  man's need
Leaving him with all his greed
She flew with mighty wings
And took back all those
  beautiful things.

Paul Thompson, 14, Jamaica

Some genius will build a giant bubble over the United States. And our factories will pollute outside the bubble so the air inside is fresh. In 25 years I don't think anything will be the same. People will have huge noses and lungs, because of the debris that comes with the oxygen.

LKH, 15, America

I think that the twenty-first century will be over-populated, over-polluted and in a big mess. There will even be mess coming out of the taps. I am sorry to say it but I think the next century will be a disaster.

Louise Lander, 15, Australia

PLEASE DONT HURT ME.

Peter Weppener, 10, South Africa

The Earth is a planet,
Which revolves round the sun,
And it's very important
To every one.
But to people
Who gaze from outer space,
It's a dirty,
Horrible, ugly, place.
Industries belch out
Polluting smoke,
Not worried about
People who might even choke.
They're not interested in spoiling the land so sunny,
All they want
Is money, money, money.

Jane Baker, 14, United Kingdom

Jane Baker

OH my God not an other tanker

David Piper

In my heart I think that if all the children around the world would help, we could do something about this disgusting air, water and ground. I think the chldren have to do something about it.

Poluting the air is one of the most horrible things to do for your world. Have you seen the water of the seas, full of rubish, oil and junk? If we go on like that the animals of the seas would die and we will never have the buitiful wonders of the seven seas.

So if we all try very hard we would make this world so much better than it already is.

Roya Rezakhanloull, 11, Iran

The only way a person can put the world right, is to start in his own country. I think Tonga is not a very clean place, but I will help my country to be clean by picking up rubbish whenever I see any and I will not throw paper, tin cans and bottles around.

Liane Mateaki, 11, Tonga

Being an island, we depend greatly on the sea for our food, but again here some thoughtless people will in time cause this rich source to be depleted by the wrongful use of dynamite for fishing and ultimatly the destruction of reefs and marine life.

The new vogue is for black coral jewelry and divers have to go to great depths to bring up this new 'black gold' to fashion into pendants and other ornaments, but in so doing they are stripping our reefs of their natural beauty and in time it could affect it permanently.

Divers and fishermen alike are responsible for slowly depleting our sea of sea-eggs by gathering them out of season, and of turtles by spearing the very young ones and killing the adult ones when they come on the beaches to lay their eggs. This rich source of protein is being threatened, not only here, but world wide and we must be made aware of the danger and pass the necessary laws to protect them.

Elizabeth Kirton, 14, Barbados

Giant supertankers, weighing over two hundred thousand tons, float like huge ecological bombs on our oceans.

Rajesh Kumar Patel, 15, Fiji

I would try to take all the oil off the sea and then boats and ships can sail safely.

David Johnson, 11

WHEN MORNING FILLS MY WHOLE BEING, I'D LIKE TO GET
DRUNK WITH THE PUREST OF DEW'S AIR.
   AND, WHEN I LOOK AT ALL THE CHIMNEYS, AND ALL THE THICK,
BLACK SMOKE, I PITY THE SUN AND I PITY MYSELF
CHOKED BY THE SMOKE.
SO, THEN, I EASE DOWN MY SHUTTERS, ON WHICH I
PAINTED THE BLUE SKY AND LITTLE CLOUDS, LIKE IT
USED TO BE, AND I CLOSE MYSELF IN MY TINY
SHELL OF DREAMS.

Marie-Jeanne Lecca, Romania

Nature is very important to all of us — physically as well as mentally. We would not have food without Nature and we would not be mentally balanced without Nature.

How could I contribute to protecting Nature?

I don't destroy plants by spreading poisons in Nature, for instance. Plants produce oxygen without which we could not breathe. Every nutrition chain begins with a combining plant, too.

I don't litter Nature with garbage.

I don't pollute water.

I don't pollute air by using my private car when going to work in the future. One diesel bus pollutes the air much less than 20 to 30 private cars.

If all other people followed these rules: I don't destroy, I don't litter, I don't pollute, I don't spoil, the future generations could walk in a wild forest or on a green meadow, swim in unpolluted water and breathe fresh air.

Petteri Takkunen, 14, Finland

Man before 'progress'

How did the world come to be so full of troubles and corruption? It is man who, to prove his ability and out of sheer pride and greed, uses all his energy and possibilities to invade planets, to build monstrous buildings in valleys, and remove mountains from their natural locations. The man of today has become completely surrounded by machines. He has become so involved in technology, that this has caused his separation from others of his kind.

The educated man of today lives a life of isolation. He is with other fellow-workers, with his friends and his family, yet, inwardly he is separate from all of them, for they cannot understand each other anymore. They know about all the wires and screws of computers, but not about the feelings and needs of themselves.

The technical societies are too well organized with definite limits, levels, ways and principles, that soon limit human relationships. Have you ever been to a village where almost everything is natural? I have been to villages, and I have seen not only the beauty of the stream with living fish in it, not only the freshness of the summer breeze, but the depth and pleasantness of human relationships there. I have seen men and women who speak, laugh or shout at each other, from the depth of their hearts. The children of the village wander and play free from the imprisoning strands of science and its poisonous products.

They might not have colour televisions, but they have many friends, who can always be found to play with, in the muddy road. In comparison, what does a city-child have to play with, to experience the years of innocent childish wonders with? Is it not true that he hardly has anything or anyone except the television set and his speaking and walking toys? Have you ever watched the faces of 'modern' children? Have you noticed the wave of indifference, dissatisfaction and disillusionment in their faces? It is sad to think of the future of these unfortunate children.

Despite having hundreds of examples before us the youngsters rush towards drugs and rebellions, which have overtaken the citizens of modern cities, we ignore them all.

At the same time, the less advanced countries tend to forget about their culture and needs, desperately and helplessly following the advanced countries. They hysterically strive to reach what they have reached, never asking themselves whether or not what other countries have reached is, in fact, what they want to reach too.

The world has become a merry-go-round, around which mankind is turning in circles. This has been created by man's stupidity and will eventually lead to his own destruction.

There is still enough time to save humanity. Men must try and stop all that is threatening their existence: pollution, violence and the uncloseness of human-beings: their mistrusting each other and their isolation. World energy may be used to bring the health that does not come from pills and injections, but from a freedom of mind of inner happiness. Technology can be used, but only to a certain extent. It may provide food, shelter, physical health to people, but it can never nourish their souls. This is why all mental problems of today are created. Human beings can nourish their souls only through relationships with others, love and inner enlightment. If this cannot be accepted with technology, then the latter must be abolished. For man should not risk and give up his own existence for the sake of that of technology. The younger generations must be helped to trust others, to regain their lost hopes for a better future.

Atoosha Pezeshgpour, 16, Iran

Michael Hardwick, 12, Australia

now the world is really modernized, machines, computers and auto-mobiles are taking the place of us atomic bombs are destroying our country scenes and soon our planet earth will look no better than a piece× piece of half eaten cheese.......

I, a prospective medical student, would rather amputate hatred, than cure cancer; for what is the use of having healthy people, if they hate each other?

Laila Risgallah, 19, Egypt

I sometimes think what would happen if Wordsworth would come again? Today we live amidst the smoke of factories and not the sweet scent of roses.

Today the greenery and beauty of nature have just become the subjects of fairy tales or the subjects of paintings. Such paintings are fixed in the frame and kept in our dining-rooms on which there is ·. thick layer of carbon particles.

Friends I would only say as Lawrence has said, 'For God's sake, let us be man, not monkeys minding machines'.

Sanjiv M Mehta, 15, India

I am convinced that a solution can only be found if we reorientate our loves and motivations in order to achieve genuine progress and not progress in the old sense, that is, one born out of the basic western philosophy that 'Man is part of nature and nature exists to serve man, God's crowning achievement'. This inherent belief by western man has resulted in contempt for less technologically advanced communities like the 'hunter and gatherer' communities In pursuit of his mastery over nature western man has pushed some of his ideas down our throats so that some people like myself lead complicated lives which he regards as perfect and legitimate. He has manipulated the thinking of youth so that it has come to accept that 'some men are more equal than others' and has relegated me to a position of subservience. Through indoctrination, he has become more powerful – militarily, economically, culturally and otherwise. Throughout the world he has imposed his 'right' values on other people and this evangelical fervour has enabled him to win over all to the view that the pursuit of material things is the noblest thing in life.

Metlhaetsile Leepile, 19, Botswana

The world, in its original, natural state was a beautiful, lush, peaceful place — until man came along. The price for being the most intelligent, advanced creature is high. We have polluted, destroyed, even desecrated.

For many years now, man has ceased to work for the good of the world. Politics has entered in too strongly, with each country inventing better ways to destroy each other rather than working together for world understanding.

I feel more of the poorer countries should be encouraged to develop while some rich countries are too rich and powerful for their own good.

R Coe, 14

What good the rockets brought from the moon. Bits of 'Rocks!' Can you imagine such great scientists on the moon collecting rocks which has no value in the world for there is an excess of it. Just for those rocks, they throw away millions of dollars. I would almost fill myself with pride imagining the same amount of money being spent on helping the poor.

Kishore Kumar, 16, Fiji

Man has developed over the centuries into the modern machine — capable of destroying and of building, of killing and of giving life, of making light and of turning to darkness. These human machines who provide the light of life for thousands are themselves blind.

In his never-ending quest for progress, man has many times changed into an animal.

Today he has become a machine. Tomorrow may see no living organism on earth. The environment that was once clean and green, is now grey and blotched. Much of the once living is now dead, some are even now dying. Our future is no future. It will be a faint echo of happier days. It will be the grey wisp of smoke left after a blazing fire. It will be the shattered wreck of a machine left from an explosion after an age of the modern sciences.

It is not too late.

Even now, a few humanitarians are working to save mankind, are striving to heal the wounds of countless wars, of ambitions that shatter the world.

Ariel Lichtenstein

Our goals must be not to conquer the universe, or to upraise our prestige by winning wars, but to conquer poverty, and to uplift humanity from humiliating death.

Nazhat Shameem, 16, Fiji

Famine is menacing the densely populated part of the world, crime is increasing, religion is deteriorating, civil wars and wars between nations continue, diseases in the poor countries still exist, all these despite the advanced technology.

Roy Rahardja, Indonesia

Redevelopment is a word which has been used for a long time, to mean destroying a beautiful old building to build an ugly square house with square rooms and square this and that.

Let's start building houses that look like houses, not space age tin cans.

John Allam, 12, United Kingdom

Nalân Ozker, 13, Turkey

We have crushed the ideals of humanity under scientific achievements. I believe that machines are not sufficient to compensate the deficiency of love and happiness.

Sanjiv M Mehta, 15, India

Most of the countries are trying to show how much they know by constructing powerful machines or bombs instead of making things that can help not only themselves but the whole world.

If Africa or America is asked she would say that she likes to be the toughest in the world and the same case applies to the other Continents. But lets take some years to come when the poor contries will have some progress and they also want to show their power. Or, the whole world wants to show their power — that is, America makes something that can pollute almost whole of Africa, Africa makes something that can destroy the whole of America and Russia makes somethng that can pollute the air at the Ocean. Then the whole world will collapse since each Continent wants to show how powerful it is.

George Mwangi, Kenya

The world itself is a beautiful place. But with the presence of man on its face, it is different. The world becomes a combination of man and earth. Therefore, the beauty of the world now lies in the harmony between man and earth. But because the presence of man himself affects the earth, this new kind of beauty solely depends on what man does to it.

Ari Mudiharto, Indonesia

Oh world, you stand beneath a heavy load.
We people were made cleverer than each and everything on you.
Even yourself.
Why can't we who are clever make the world good? For it feeds us with its natural vegetation.
The white man thinks he was made to be the master of a black man.
Look! We can't even make peace between ourselves.

Johannes Mothupi, 15, Botswana

Throwing bricks through the windows of shops and houses. It is people who created these problems. Pollution is a bad thing, people, people again created these problems. People do not care any more, they just throw their Rubbish into the water.

Michael Jeffrey, United Kingdom

… by so writing I mean no love is going on among countries and among people, but Lovers this world has not changed, but the dwellers who are in it have changed.

Raphael Mutisya, Kenya

**Of all the creatures that creep, swim or fly,
peopling the earth, the waters and the sky,
from Rome to Iceland, Paris to Japan,
I really think the greatest fool is man.**

Ornan Yotrath, Iran

Nobody is ignorant of the consequences of progress upon today's humanity. The whole universe has been turned upside down, transformed under the whip of progress.
Science is, before everything else, the first instigator of progress. It has improved man's standard of living, and has increased the demographic curve of the world; which leads to problems of overpopulation. Mechanization brought the inclination to speed, the errors and misdeeds which we acknowledge, with the great thinker Alain: 'It impoverishes us, but also brutalizes the people which will soon be lead by the rhythm of business to the diligent stupidity of the bees'.
The invention of nuclear weapons is increasing rapidly, and is a real nightmare for young people. In industrialized countries, pollution is a serious problem. In most African countries, one is confronted by the generation gap, unemployment, juvenile delinquency, economic crises. Today's man hates loneliness, seeks comfort near the 'musical boxes', or in front of a screen. He is afraid of himself. We can see that man's inventions come from his inquisitiveness. Scientism has taken an infernal rhythm over the last fifty years.
Alexis Carrel in 'Man, that unknown creature', shows us that the knowledge of man is ever less sound than the knowledge of nature. The science of human behaviour is only at its beginnings. Progress doesn't keep the same pace.
My wish is that progress might become the flight of a family in which each member tries to drag his neighbour along instead of a galloping of ruffians, in which the most disfavoured are left to their fate. For a better progress, we need adaptation, harmonization and equilibration. Man has sufficiently moulded, handled, transformed nature, even to its core, but never has he transformed himself. I am not interested in the transformation brought to man by the fruit of his invention, but a transformation in which man *makes* himself. When the walk becomes laborious, when the giants slower the pace, it is good to put back in order what has been lent to us. Far from closing my eyes to the benefits of progress, I wanted to quote an African saying: 'When the flame is high, it must have a thought for water'. We know that the higher ones goes, the harder one's fall will be. I think it is time to think about the future of progress, so as not to beget a sickly and hopeless generation.

Zongo Marou, Upper Volta

From the wilderness man built this world,
Carved paths and harnessed forces that
  were thought forever wild,
Made reality from dreams, and dreamed
  anew.
With toil and ingenuity
With hope and sweat and pain
Man civilised this earth;
He made all that he is, and all he will be,
To make a better world ~
Man has progressed.
Now, who will civilize man?

Irene Sandyord, Barbados

The world is extremely complicated
and is full of violence and corruption.
For this reason I would be hard put to
find a way of improving it.
When one first thinks about it, one
would almost immediately say,
'Simple! Just disarm and destroy every
weapon a country has!'
But this would mean a mass peace
movement involving many countries.
Even then people all over the world
would start a sort of 'black market' on
arms, bombs and other weapons which
would be similar to the drug problem
we have now.
I think this 'putting the world to rights'
is an impossible task for any human
being because the roots of the bad
things of this world are in peoples'
minds. It is one person's, or many
peoples' attitudes to something which
causes so many of the problems,
whether they be political or racial or
whatever.
Therefore I think it an impossible task
for any one person to improve or put
the world to rights.
Andrew Collinson, 13, United Kingdom

The world goes on with so many
injustices, envies, violences ... but who
runs this world? Beings from other
planets? No. It is men who run it, with
their reason and intelligence.
Glemencia Patal, 15, Guatemala

Andrew Mair

91

I long for security

In the settlement (if you can call it that)
  where we live, the shacks are made
  of tin picked up from the street
The shacks look like patch quilts
  as they stand forlornly in the sun
The pungent smells of excrement
  and filth fill my nostrils
Children fight and squabble
  over who is the richest
At mealtimes they return only to ask
  sadly,
'Is it black beans again, Ma?'
Then show me a good mother
  whose heart does not ache when her
  child asks for more to eat
And she has nothing.

Hunger is something only the hungry
  can feel
Thus others do not know
  the cries of pain
The nights of endless dreams of food
Digging in garbage cans
  during the day.

Odille Danford, 15, Fiji

To the Great Powers and Rich Nations

It is with great feelings I have to address
you about the living conditions of the
majority of the population of the
world. Most people do not even have
one square meal even once a day. They
do not get jobs so that they cannot drive
away wants from their doors. Even if
they get jobs, remuneration is not
equal for the work done. They are
unable to provide their children with
food. Some of them, toddlers aged 6 to
8, are sent out to do odd jobs to earn
their bread. The people have no cloth
to cover themselves. The males have
only one loin cloth and a small towel.
The women have only one cheap saree.
Some even do not have cholis. These
people do not have any dress like shirts,
bedsheets etc. to protect themselves
against the weather, cold or hot. They
do not even have a spare dress to wear
after bathing.
Worst of all is shelter. They have no
house. Some of them have to live in
huts on the banks of rivers built of
materials that easily catch fire. In rains
and floods they are carried away. These
sufferings cannot be described. These
half-starved, half dead and uneducated
are easily prone to disasters. There have
not sufficient hospitals to give medical
treatment. Most of the people are.
uneducated. Because of the poverty
they are reluctant to send their children
to school. Instead they send their
children to eke-out their food. Even
adults are not educated. Woes of the
people cannot be described sufficiently
on paper. Big nations which are rolling
in wealth and luxury, especially the
USA, can, if they wished to, take heart
the sufferings of these people, and do
something to save them.

S Gomathi, India
(An orphaned girl
in a large Ghandhian school)

We were hungry and shivering. We
begged for a piece of bread.
The people gave for the refugees
whatever they had. But we were
thousands.
And it was that day when the first
parcels began to arrive. They called
them the parcels of love.
We were standing in a queue. At last
they gave to me my own parcel. I ran
quickly to my tent, I opened it. A lovely
dress, a pairs of shoes, what nice
clothes. And some sweets, some
biscuits.
I looked at them and tears were coming
out from my eyes. How good it is to
find people who think of others who
live in misery. How different should be
the world if everybody thought the
poors of all the world,
Happiness should rule on earth.

Soula Kyriakou, 10, Cyprus

If I were President of Colombia I would
build houses where the street children
could be educated as they are in the
Club Michin Houses and they would
not be allowed to inject themselves
with drugs or smoke marijuana. And I
would provide wholesome amusement
better than drinking beer and spirits.

O B Fernandez, 14, Colombia
Ed: This child lived on the street
before being cared for by the Club Michin,
supported by Oxfam

We were hungry and shivering. We begged for a piece of bread.

Soula Kyriakou, 10, Cyprus

Soula Kyriakou

Gulsim Dolgun, 15, Turkey

93

Hi-jack

Karin Ramskogler

It is Tuesday, the 24th of March, 1980, 3 p.m. From Kennedy Airport in New York Jet-Airliner 793 is taking off. All seats are taken with people full of hope, full of wishes and plans, but also full of worries. Soon the plane is high up in the air, flying quietly. Deep below the country unrolls like a grand film! In the middle of the plane a newly married couple is sitting. Both young people enjoy their honeymoon trip to Europe. For months they have been saving money and they have been looking forward to it. Now their dream has become reality.

Not far from them a student is longing to come home again to West-Germany to his parents, his sisters and brothers. He has studied with very good success. How proud his parents will be! Beside him an afflicted lady is leaning in her seat. She has decided to get a divorce from her husband and now she wants to go back to her mother in Frankfurt. A businessman has got good news; he can settle a profitable business in London and his son is allowed to accompany his father for the first time on his business trip. An actress is intensively studying and repeating her part . . . The monotonous noise of the machines mixes with a deadened jumble of voices, hostesses are busy serving little refreshments to the passengers, people are relaxing, they feel quite comfortable.

There – a man approaches the cockpit. Excited voices are to be heard. Some minutes later the loudspeaker announces: 'We are compelled to make an intermediate landing. Please, keep quiet!'. The pilot's voice sounds oppressed. The stranger puts pressure on him. Nobody talks about it, but everybody knows and feels the tremendous tension. – Silence again.

The newly married couple press to each other. How good that they are together! 'If I could only see my parents, my homecountry once more', the student is thinking. 'How sorry I am that I was angry with my husband. Perhaps we could try to live together once more. I will annul our divorce', the lonely lady meditates. 'My wife will worry about John and me', the businessman considers. He doesn't care about his business any more. If only John could be saved! The actress is absent-mindedly staring at her papers.

'Please, keep quiet!' the pilot's voice once more is thundering through the stillness. Suddenly a woman is yelling. She has got a nervous breakdown. At that moment there is a dazzling light like a flash of lightning and a fearful crash . . .

Next day people could read in the papers: 'Jet-Airliner 793 of the American Airline was blown up by a terrorist yesterday at 4 pm. All passengers are dead'.

How could this happen? – And it happens again and again. I can't understand why people can become so terribly unfeeling. With one blow they destroy so many human lives, so many expectations, so much happiness.

Karin Ramskogler, 16, Austria

I am a young boy from East Harlem in Manhatten, New York. I have seen burglary after burglary, and vandalism taking place. I have lived in a slum all my life and it seems that I live in a world of hate. I have had friends who have been the victims of a burglary, from what they have told me, its not a good feeling, your house full in the morning and returning and finding nothing. I have seen vandals destroying a building from top to bottom, taking every useful piece of appliance and destroying it. Hate is something everyone has, I know because I have people who hate me. But still I do nothing to harm them. Living in a slum is really no different than living in a high class area, because everywhere in the world you will find Burglary, Vandalism and Hate.

Carlos Meletiche, USA

Last week one of my friends' father died after being injured while somebody tried to kill him. Now the friend who was schooling has to leave school and work for his family. The fellow's studies have vanished just because of the murderer and the whole family has to suffer now. What happened to the criminal? He is sent to jail just for a few years. In the jail the criminal has been fed well. He had a place to sleep and live. That's no punishment. Today in the jails it is too comfortable for lazy fellow to live in.
Nowadays people steal or commit any other kind of crimes just to enter the jail where they will be fed and have clothes to wear while living his own life is boring and too complicated.

Deokumar Singh, 15, Fiji

When one thinks of the turmoil, crimes, murders etc........one is gripped suddenly by fear.

Janet Curtis, 14, Jamaica

I would remove crime because a lot of people are afraid to go out at night alone and too many people walk with fear inside them.

Felicia Gaskin, 13, Barbados

Rape should be eliminated. There is some excuse for a man if he is mentally insane, but none at all if he is sane. I honestly don't think men understand how hurt, shocked and humiliated a girl feels when she has been raped. If they did I don't think there would be half so many rape cases. Besides the feeling of deep mental and physical shock and hurt, what happens if she becomes pregnant? She is going to have to make the decision of if she is going to bear the baby and bring it up and be saddled with it and reminded of its dreadful origin all her life or if she will give it up to be adopted — and be reminded of the child — *her* child which she gave away or if she should have an abortion and know that she has destroyed a part of her — a life. If men thought of all this there would be very few rapes.

Sally Harris, 15, Barbados

Dearbhla Gowen, Ireland

The world is a sad place,
To survive we have to kill,
We shoot the fox
We chase the deer
We arrow the birds from year
 to year,
That beautiful coat was once a fox.
Alive with family so dear,
That deer who's head hangs
 on the wall
Did have a heart after all.
And the sweet birds that once flew,
Life will not change, NEVER.

Jane Scanlon, 10 United Kingdom

Guissou Jahangiri
14 years old
Rustam Abadian International School
Tehran, Iran.

My World
=========

Right now I'm sitting on top of the world.
watching and wandering about this mysterious
planet called: EARTH

I look at my right, to a continent
called Asia.

I see poverty: men, woman, children all
crying of hunger, their bodies covered by little
pieces of cloth, in the cold and hot —
 nothing more.

I see War, men dieying, houses
collapsing — fire — bomb, guns —— blood
 everywhere.

Man's cruelty towards his own
 race —— people being ignored,
being left alone. Why? oh why? Just
because of their colour?

What is this? Why is man so selfish?
Racial Discrimination

This makes me feel very sad, so I
turn my head, towards a nother continent.
but I can't see anything, It's this layer of
smoke —— POLLUTION

Now, when will this all end!
When will man become free of
all his problems? WHEN?

It is a vast world resting on me — a whole globe: and I am a midget beneath it. So I lie still under it — and let it crush me.

Gotswamang Maphanyane, 16, Botswana

Alone on the beach
Away from the world's reach.
Alone by the sea,
All alone with me.
I look for snails and shells.
I sit there watching the tide go by
Wanting to cry.

David Mogull, USA

I hope others will realise, as I have, there is little hope — if any at all — that the dream of a better world will come true. There can never be a better world. Happier for some, never better. For there will be those who will continue the fight and those who will suffer for it.

John Arlita, 13, Barbados

Oh! my world, you're such a tough, boring place. No one is happy on you my world, you are such an undescribable place. Murderers are being born, they kill people. Apartheid is taking over, people are dying in many places, this really is heartbreaking. God did not create the world to become such a miserable place.

Meriam Polile, 13, Botswana

All these world problems, I cannot really say how to put them right, because after all, that is the reason they are world problems … because there is no real solution.

P. Collins, 14

Human history on the globe will certainly be destroyed because of our selfishness, and it will happen as quickly as it started. But who would care about it, thousands of years hence, in the eternal, endless space.

Pirjo Tikkanen, 17, Finland

The future had arrived

It is quite a long time since I first came here. The earth was still desolate and void then. Immense powers were fighting each other in the glowing darkness. I felt ill at ease and so I disappeared quickly.

I soon returned full of curiosity. And, behold I saw that the future had arrived, and written her history. I felt life was astir and trying to build a dwelling-place. It is good like this, I said, and remained in the world.

But when I acquainted myself with my surroundings, I soon came to realize that my idea about the good world was doomed. I wandered from one country to another, and the errors I saw and the false wellbeing made me frown.

On the morning of the first day I arrived in a big country and saw its people working hard. They were dark-skinned, and I often saw them shake their fists at their white foreman. I saw how rebellions were subdued by ruthless violence. I heard coloured people shout and demand rights which only the white people had in this country. I joined in shouting with them, but nothing essential happened, and so I wandered on to the next day, broken-hearted.

I came to a strange area. I expected to see a lot of animals. The place looked, however, most desolate and abandoned, and at last when I found a living being, I saw a man rising from the bushes and killing it as he had killed so many others before. It was growing dusk when I fled from that haunt of nightmare.

When I arrived in a city, it was night and the world was asleep. Under the dim stars I could see a dark car pulling up in front of a house. I saw two men with gloomy eyes come from the car and knock on the door of the house. And the men went in and came out again with three other men who had a scared gait. They all went into the car and drove away. The political darkness was blurring even the light of the stars. I began to follow the car with my mind full of suspicion. At dawn I saw them go into a cellar and heard the cries of the fettered men. I stopped petrified. In the freshness of the evening it was quiet at last and the two gloomy-eyed men again drove away mysteriously. The three men in their gleaming chains were never seen again.

Next day I came to a shore where there was not only a war going on between the ideologies within a state which were fighting for power but also between different states — on a psychological level. On both shores they were disguising themselves between false smiles of friendship and building arms to be ready to divert the attack of the other part at any time or to be able to attack them. At the same time great negotiations were being carried on about the limitation of armaments, and I felt I did not understand the world any longer.

Once again I tried to find something ever-lasting on the earth. I walked on and on along the coast and saw a most lovely place in the distance, and I felt a hope stirring in my chest. But what should I meet! I saw the leaves withering on the trees and the sludge flowing towards the ocean, slowly and irrevocably. I looked up the river and saw two industrial cities covered with a dirty, grey cloud. The earth and the air were giving way to progress.

Dear world, so I turned round and remained waiting like millions of others all over this globe.

Taina Kettunen, 17, Finland

Ian Donaghy, 11, United Kingdom

The world has changed from ancient to modern. The men themselves have changed. Here we are in this new world with its new things leading us no where.

Leonard Mwangi, 13, Kenya

If I ruled the world the sun would shine everyday and little warm raindrops would come down from heaven. I would be kind and loving and give lots of money to the poor. I don't rule the world and flowers die too quickly. It's dark and dingy and the showers from heaven are freezing. But who cares? Nobody cares, except me.

Julie Kemp, 11, United Kingdom

I'd like to stop everything that is not good for you. I'd stop smoking but I can't. If say no smoking they will smoke even more so I'd better keep my mouth shut. My life will be a misery if I don't stop this. I would like to stop vandalism but I can't. So.

Denise Masson, 9, United Kingdom

Soon the coal miners are going on strike. We will have no coal. I would let people have a little bit and save some. But people *will* waste these things. If there is no coal how are we going to keep warm? We could put lots of clothes on. I would go underground and see what is causing earthquakes. The world is in such a state. The countries are fighting over silly things. We hope the coal miners do not go on strike. Otherwise we will be in such a state. The world is in one great mess.

Mieka Waugh, 9, United Kingdom

There is killing and fighting and people robbing other people, and I feel so down-hearted that I am a part of this country. The Governor try so very hard to make peace in our country and still they won't help and if someone put hand and heart and help our country, well the world today would be a better place ... If all the people had faith in God and try to do the right thing, well the world would be a wonderful place. We are all one, let's make Jamaica a peaceful and loving place ... Oh please world try and do good not worse.

Sharon, 16, Jamaica

Everything sounds to easy when we talk about it, when anyone tries to change anything you find out how difficult it really is.

Jillian Moore, 14

Some people need jobs and do not get enough money. And some people are shortage of food. To many people are getting shot. Banks are getting robbed. In America there are earth-quiks and over 40,0,0 people are killed and injured like at a football match people get killed with knives and Mexico there are volcano's very dangours and over a million people get killed. And in America there are stunt men on motor-bike's and they make a round fire and go threw and kill there selfs. In London there are packerge's and blow up. In Bermuda some ships have been disapareding away and we can not find them.

*David Ballantyne, 9,
United Kingdom*

If the bombers from other countrys keep on bombing Ireland I will have to catch them. The people are bombing because they fighting over who should rule the country. The catholics or the protestants. The people in India and in Africa they are starving. There are lots of people who are going on strike because they do not want to go to work. There are some rivers that are polluted and all of our best fish are dieing. There should be more unemployment because people are not getting any money. There is a water shortage in South Wales and the ground is cracking. There is fighting in South Africa about the white people going over there. They will not allow white people in there. There are some mums and dads who throw their children out because they dont want them. There are some children who dont get presents at Christmas. In the year two thousand there will not be any petrol. There will not be any electricity because there will be a shortage. Soon we will have to make more houses because they will fall down. The Russians are bombing America and the Americans are nearly bombed out. Some people are racing up to space because there is a race up there. There are things calld flying saucers are coming down to earth. A man said he saw one when he was in his car in London.

David Baker, 8, United Kingdom

The world is in such a terrible state,
We'll go to the dogs at this rate.
Nicola Hanks, 12

Today's world is very much changed,
under any sucamstance. People of
nowadays simply they are not
respectifuly like people of last years,
espacially girls and boys. When ever
they are met by a old man or woman
they do not move to let him or her pass
they go on chatering what they wanted
to say. So I write this to acknowledge-
ment my lovely brothers and sisters to
stop this.

Raphael Mutisya, Kenya

If the state we're in gets any worse,
you'll all be crying out: 'Stop the world
I want to get off'.
Lynn Govan, 15, Iran

The world is passing a very mysterious
period.
Countries are indifferent. People are
suffering. Wars are spread all over the
countries. Misery is known to so many
people.
Kalid Ahmed Fahmy, Libya

**By the way, America, have you
done anything about your
horrific pollution problem? No, I
thought not. Cut down on your
cars, manufacture more bicycles
and let your citizens discover
what legs are.**
**England, has anything happened
about your unemployment? Why
not? You should start more
bicycle factories, and send them
to America. Russia, if you could
possibly stop sending rockets to
the moon, just for a few years,
there's time for that in the
future, but when people on your
own planet are starving it seems to
be ludicrous.**
**All you countries which are having
petty little fights, especially
Ireland, I am sick and I am tired
of Northern Ireland. You and your
cowardly bombers who kill
anyone, anywhere, for any reason.
I suppose it would be asking too
much of you to at least stop for a
while, whilst we try and put this
world right. If you are so desperate
to kill, do so later, but for now . . .
stop . . . please?**
Lynn Govan, 15, Iran

No one can put the world right. Such is its sad plight. One must have a very big broom and a much bigger mop to clean its dirt.

Alexandros Valsamidis, 9, Greece

Timbo Paul Sawadogo, 14, Upper Volta

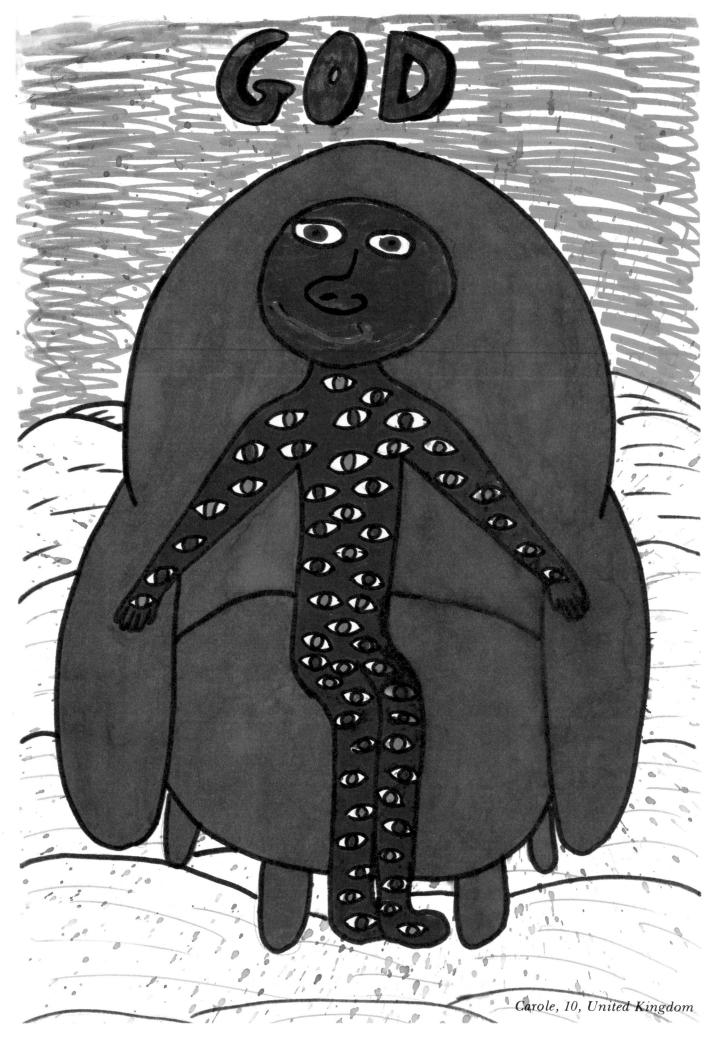

GOD

Carole, 10, United Kingdom

Oh, my God, give us a world without the evil. It is enough. No more bloodshed. No more tortures. End the wars, end the killings, end the sufferings. Send peace to the world. Spare love between people. Make all men to shake hands.
Please God, make your love wing all over the world. Send us freedom and send smiles to our faces again. Bring back our missing fathers, sons, brothers and all beloved persons.
Put under your blessed hands all orphans.
Make enemies to be friends again. Please, God, accept my prayer, and bring happiness everywhere.

Elena Orphanou, 10, Cyprus

All people walk together work together pray together for a happy pretty world.
Elicia Alleyne, 5, Trinidad

Man needs more than the satisfaction of his materialistic needs. Man is a selfish, savage and greedy animal. Religion changes this animal into a real human being. Do not think that man can rule the world without the help of God, for technology has its very dark and dangerous side.

Sami Raghda, 15, Egypt

And my poor little self am already ruling the world because I exist and add to its beauty ... I am already feeling the sweetness of walking with God!
Shahin Zeinab, 16, Egypt

The human beings have forgot the Almighty God. Instead man has accepted human wisdom and sagacity. Although man is as free as air, he under-weighs the spirital values. Sex has dominated man. Luxury, adultery, sin and evil play vital role in human life. People have become materialist.

Mohammad Ayaz, Pakistan

The church would have to abandon its traditional role of indoctrination. It would cease to exploit the people's poverty for its own ends and in particular, desist from promising people 'pie in the sky'. It would help all people to attain self-realisation. It should act as a source of unity rather than friction. Above all the church should not engender an attitude of docility which, more often than not, precedes human degradation and exploitation.

Metlhaetsile Leepile, 19, Botswana

I do not think there is a God. I have heard about God in the Bible and on television ... If there is a God I do not think he care for us because if he did during a war he would stop it. When I say prayers in school I do not mean them and I do not think God is listening.

Benjamin, 9

Religion is about love and peace. Then why do people fight and kill each other for religion.

Sossy Neredian, 17, Egypt

I would let the races of the world to follow their own religion. It would be no use of forcing the whole world to follow one religion, eg Christianity. Lets take an example of the Chinese. They are communists, yet they do not steal. They even says it is bad to insult. If I was to go to China, leave K1000.00 on a counter, it would stay there for centuries. Now we christians, we steal, insult and do all soughts of bad things yet we say we follow the commandments of God. It's obvious that there are more communists going to heaven than christians.

Bede L Mpande, 13, Zambia

So people are protesting that God does not exist and some other go to an extent of saying that Satan is not a being but the sin which people perform. Other say that God is there with his angels and Jesus and they are likely to come once and took all people for prosecution. Who are we going to belief? We better be stuck at the centre.
Samuel Wambu, Kenya

In my dream world all the children be gleaming with the light of heaven and fill the yard of the world with laughter and pleasure.

Mathusudan Mallick, India

101

Sossy Neredian

Why, oh Why?

Since the beginning of time the law of the world has been that power is the only means for survival and that one must kill and destroy the other in order to live. In the sea big fish eat small ones in order to live. It is their instinct; nobody has taught them to do it. Kindness, gentleness and pity do not survive in this world.

Where is the justice of nature? Do you call it justice to create crippled people, blind people, abnormal people who spend their lives miserably being ignored and laughed at by others? Do you call it justice to create idiots and stupid people besides intelligent ones? Do you call it justice when somebody is born in a poor family whereas others are born in rich families? What is the sin of the child to be born poor? Do you call it justice to create black, white, red and yellow people? What have the red and the black ones done to be despised by the whites? Their only sin is that God has created them coloured.

I would like to tell some words to my people. Why don't they try to spend their lives pleasantly? Why do they fight and kill each other for a piece of land or wealth or ambition that when they die they won't be able to take with them? Why don't they try to help each other, forgive each other, love each other? Why don't they try to make the world a better place? Why? Why?

Sossy Neredian, 17, Egypt

What's happening to this world? Why can't people live in harmony caring for each other instead of listening to the news of war, where thousands of people are dying in hunger and distress all over the world, and why can't these countries with plenty of money share with the less fortunate? Instead they hang onto every single penny, scared it might be taken from them.

Honestly — I really think this world will end up having greedy men, snobs and hypocrites even though it isn't far from it now. Why can't we live in harmony, all it needs is thought, deep thought, I wonder if any of these people who think themselves 'almighty' ever stopped to wonder what life really is.

Sharlene Farrell, 13, New Zealand.

Make our hopes come true

The world, living and beautiful,
contains the elements of Paradise,
the yellow, green, red colours
the balance of nature.

But why do the people,
    to whom God has given
the world to rule,
make life difficult for our
    neighbours
and trample on a dandelion?

And why do
so many people in Chile
so many children
    in the Near East and Ethiopia
have to suffer
because of lust for power?

And why are
so many children in India and Africa
starving
because of ignorance?

And why do
so many Negroes in South Africa
    and North America
as well as our own Gipsies
have to suffer
because of their race?

And why do
I, a European,
live in a constant fear
because of threat of war?

Man,
ruler of species,
    grow wise and abolish
from the earth
ambition,
ignorance,
racial hatred and
the threat of war,
for your own sake.

Since you have
    the power and the strength and
the need to make the world better.

Matti Heikkilä, 17, Finland

This earth of ours is a deathly black silhouette,
This world that we live in is a sinister world,
A world of confounding tussle,
Where nothing is cheap and good,
Where everything is cheated for food,
Where no hearts are wholly satisfied.
But you, mighty Creator, how would you make this bloody world a
    better place to live in?
Why are there people in this world who bring inflation and cause misery?
Why are there people who starve and die?
Why can't there be a new, a brand new world?
A world where there will be no such thing as a boundary line?
Why can't all black and white and brown live one life with joy
    and glory,
And share their happiness and sorrow?
Why can't everybody sing,
Like brothers and make everyday worth living?
I hope the Great God has heard me.

Anita Seth, 13, Iran

Tania Eber, 9

Nurnihal Horsa, 15, Turkey

The Aftermath

The dawn comes
But is it day?
The dark empty shell called earth
   remains still.
An eerie wind catches the dust —
   and carries it yonder.
Silence fell long ago
When the sun left the sky.
A bomb came and went
And we were no more.
But our spirits are alive.
They shall stay for eternity
Calling and whispering the secrets of a
   dead and long forgotten planet!!
               Marie Sawer, 11, Australia

The world I used to know

I look around, and amazed I see
A huge desert with no human being,
The sky is red and pouring down on
me,
It's almost dark like a blood sea.

The fields are burnt also the trees,
A shrunken branch is bending
   down on me,
I'm frightened, I look around,
   but all that I can see
Is a blood sky that's pouring
   down on me.

I run, I scream, but no sound I can hear;
The moon, the stars, the sun
   have disappeared,
The silence is so hard for me, so

I give up, I sit down,
And hopeless now I ask:
'Where is the world I used to know?
Where are the trees, the flowers
   and the bees?
The yellow fields, the burning sun
   above,
The bright blue sky,
   the pretty birds that fly?
They often sang for me.
Where have they gone?
What made them disappear?
               Atanasiu Lucia, Romania

The 'World Powers' store the end of the world.

John C Khumalo, 16, Botswana

105

Marie-Jeanne Lecca, 17, Romania

The Struggle

I see a world which is bleak as mist;
  being symbolic of
Civilization's foolish fist.
It has no beauty nor any charm,
  for after the struggle,
Nature retreated its mighty arm.

I can see the oceans filled with
  floating carcasses; of once giant
Living things now in total darkness.
Pitiful are the forests, as if stricken
  by disease; barren as
The deserts with signs of former trees.

The cities are not flourishing
  just like they used to be; there is
No work, there is no food,
  there is no industry.
The sky is not blue and plentiful,
  like in its former years;
It is now grey and eerie,
  filled with long abandoned hopes,
And painful endless tears.

So what have they accomplished
  in this productivity? A world that's
Dead and dreary, with no right place
  to be.
So who then won this struggle?
  'No one' is the reply.
Man destroys himself and fails
  to reason why.

David Sobel, USA

I looked for the sand, for the sound
    of millenary shards,
I forced my eyes into the depths.
The dark winds, carriers of thick,
    black smoke,
Laughed wildly and frighteningly,
And my heart, my poor heart
Was trying to shed its crazy tears.
But the seagulls have gone,
The seagulls have gone.

Sometimes in pilgrimage I go
To stop at the limpid edges
    of the cliffs.
I pause in the land I know so well,
Where the sun pulsates
Below the peel of juicy fruit.
I sink within the perspective spaces
    of the sky.
I bathe my eyes
In the white undefiled flight
    of the seagull,
And stand both young and old,
In the chilly whistling of the wind
    of time.

You must believe in a future
With which to paint the sea you
    dream of.
I pity you, for I dread how few can
    do it.
For the seagulls have gone,
The seagulls have gone.
        Marie-Jeanne Lecca, 17, Romania

We may have to tell our grandchildren
about the beautiful world we used to
have in our young days. Then grass was
green on the pastures where the cattle
were grazing. We may have to tell them
fairy tales about happy people
watching the purple sun set behind an
azure horizon, about the time when the
three short words 'I love you' really
meant something.
        Pirjo Tikkanen, 17, Finland

To a child in twenty years

You asked if there was ever a time
the world was at peace. No, my
child, not ever that I remember.
Not in my time, not in your
grandparents' time, not even
before that. 'Will there ever be
such a time?' I wish I *could* say yes,
but I'll never be sure. I wish I
could tell you why it's this way, I
wish I could make you understand.
You are suffering now, suffering
the consequences of past hatreds
cultivated before you were born. It
is *my* fault, my fault and the fault of
all those men and women who,
twenty years ago, did not think of
you, who tried to settle their
problems the wrong way, who let
their hate and jealousy and
prejudice overcome them.
Hate . . . that's why six million
Jews were slaughtered in the
Second World War. But you
wouldn't know about that, or
about the Irish religious conflicts
that defy the very meaning of
the religions for which they
are fighting! Oh no, you wouldn't
understand how power and greed
dominate men; how wars come
about, and with them grief,
so much tragedy . . . torture,
starvation, ruin of mind and body,

death! . . . No, you have not
experienced these. You only know
fear.
I wanted to give you the peace and
happiness which I briefly knew
in my childhood, before our
nation, too, became involved in
war's destruction. For you I
wanted friendship and love, and
boundless joy! But I have failed
you . . . look at us now . . .
What can we do, you ask? If only I
knew! No, people don't suddenly
become good, I'm sorry . . . I
know its hard for you to
understand; but its really all up
to you. You can't perfect the world,
but you can make it better, yes!
Oh God, that must be possible!
Now is the time to begin
reconstructing the damaged bridges
of friendship and understanding.
Always try to understand why
people act as they do, and never
let power and wealth lure you. The
only wealth worth having is
peace, and that is what we lack.
Rebuilding may take centuries, but
isn't it worth it, knowing that
sometime in the future the world
could be at peace? Perhaps your
children's children may have
what was meant for *you!*
Make no mistakes, my child, the
world cannot keep paying.
        Lisa Cole, 15, Barbados

My Rules For

My first rule would be that all sweet firms should be closed down to save money on dental surgery.
My second rule would be that children do not get told off for breaking rules which some adults break but do not get told off for.
My third rule would be that the news would be left out on TV to make room for something less sad.
My last rule would be that the English language stuck to its own rules.

David Wheeler, 11, United Kingdom

Kai Ranta-Knuuttila, 12, Finland

I hope for the day when the wonderful treasure of books will be shared by everyone.

Capra Victor, 15, Romania

Create thought-provoking sensation; Don't create emotion-provoking situation.
Smile in success; smile in sorrow; smile in pleasure. Don't expect respect without offering it.

V Malarvizhi, India

The world would be a much happier place to live in if we stopped complaining when things don't work out right.

Frances Meehan, 12, Eire

Respect women — they are the builders of society.

Steve Francis, 10, Trinidad

All women must think theirselves worth the value of a pearl, in the sight of men.

Jannett Pusey, 16, Jamaica

Everybody must go to school, and learn to do Modern Maths, because in the shops now it is Modern Maths they count in.

Titilayo Adebanjo, 9, Nigeria

All of these world problems must be faced with the utmost seriousity.

Triono Prasodjo, Indonesia

I would make that the uncivilated people make civilated.

Octavio Arrioloa, 9, Spain

I would try to make everyone believe in humanity, because a human being is somehow a very delicate thing.

Toro Arnold Motiki, 15, Botswana

The streets will be paved and places will not be dusty. The towns will have clean streets and nice roads. There should not be beggars. Towns and cities and villages will have things like electricity.

Alusantu Koroma, 15, Sierra Leone

Today's World

I would not allow hippie girls and boys around the world.

Miriam Nthaga, 14, Botswana

There should be no beating up old ladies.
There should be no more budgets.

Mandy Tora, 10, United Kingdom

Anyone who goes on strike should be replaced by someone on the dole.

Richard Middleton, United Kingdom

You must never fiddle people that cannot read.
You must always help your mother.

Susan Atabaki, Iran

No more factories that durt the rivers!

Olga Abasolo, 10, Spain

Thy shalt not have inflation on thy world.
Thy shalt not be ruled by strange mechanisms.
Thy shalt not drink before driving a automobile.
Thy shalt not hurt or make fun of foreigners from different countries.

Paul Torretti, 11, Australia

When you meet an adult carrying something big you must help him. Everyone you meet you must greet him, even when he is dirty. This is good manners and it shows us how to respect.

Theresa Ramsden, 14, Botswana

Always try to wake up on the right side every morning, and — if not, please ... do not be grumpy, grabby and mischievous.

Lurene Gardner, 16, Jamaica

Thou shall not vandel.
Thou shall not have more than one automobile.

Luciana Colameo, 12, Australia

I would stop the people from making cigarettes because they make me cofe.

Andrew Newman, 8, United Kingdom

It should be a compulsory task to produce food. Every man must care for plants.

Murali Adak, India

If everybody appreciated great people's ideas the world would be better.

Didem Uzumcu, 15, Turkey

Don't let a car ran over you!
Help your mummy or Daddy.

Nuria Munoz, 9, Spain

Smiles would make part of an everyday face. It would be so nice that when one person smiles the others find themselves smiling as well. When one frowns do not be surprised if the world walks frowning.

Karen Burke, 14, Barbados

Value sincerity beyond all things.

Ingrid Kramer, 14, Netherlands

Help lost people find their way.

Denise Styles, 7, New Zealand

Every child should have a home.

Victoria Hamilton, 9, United Kingdom

Don't rubbish our beautiful land.

Belinda Kershaw, 12, Australia

For five weeks in a year I would make men and boys do all the housework.

Sally Epps, 11

109

A list of 'My Ten Rules for Today's World'

Honour the human rights. Every human being has the right to food, dwelling, work and education, besides many other basic needs, which have all been listed in the UN declaration of human rights. Thus you can demand such rights, but you have to grant them to all the others as well, disregarding age, race and sex. Oppression of every kind, inequality and the restriction of the freedom of speech violate human rights. One really cannot decide in advance how one is born. Why not, then, be equal to each other?

Know your responsibility. You have rights and you have certain liberties, but you must also have a sense of responsibility. When you become an adult, the responsibility is moved from the shoulders of your parents to those of your own. As a grown-up person you must be prepared to make independent decisions and bear the responsibility. You will have to realize your own burden as a human being. It is up to you to accept the responsibility for nature preservation, world catastrophes and the welfare of other nations.

Help those in need. Help your brother, your sister, your friend at times of difficulty and worry. Listen to another human being, comfort him and support him; it is easier together to solve the problems. Try, to the best of your ability, to sustain those in financial difficulties at home or abroad. You may sometimes need help yourself; why not treat the others as you would expect them to treat you.

Value other people's attitudes and opinions. Your own ideas need not be the absolutely correct ones. Somebody else can be more familiar with some particular problem, and he may well have more justified views than you. Listen to his ideas, they may give rise to new questions and answers. When you study questions from different angles you will discover new details, and perhaps, only after that, can you expect justification of your own views. **Acquire knowledge** and use it wisely. You may have to decide about matters and adopt attitudes towards other people's views. To be able to act right you should know what decisions are made and why, and what possible results the decisions may involve. Being well conversed with the facts your influence will be more valuable in driving through the rights of other people and your own.

Abide by laws and regulations. Legislation is not there only to be obeyed; it also gives security to everybody. An organized society cannot exist without restrictions that have been agreed upon. There are, however, laws that violate human rights, and such laws should be abolished as quickly as possible. Everybody should have the chance of contributing to the amending of legislative defects and shortcomings.

Preserve nature. Nature is a very important part of our surrounding, it is an important source of energy and raw materials; thus it must be protected at all times. Pollution must be prevented, and the errors of past generations adjusted. Think how you use nature and her gifts, nature is vitally important for man.

Aim at peace. Peace is a target well worth striving towards – but not with weapons. A struggle for peace begins at home, at school, at work. Live at peace with your fellow people and settle the difficulties and quarrels talking. Work for international co-operation and peace.

Accept yourself as you are. Know your own weaknesses and assets, but do not despise or underestimate your talents and your strength. Always strive towards better things, be sufficiently humble to put right your mistakes, try to improve yourself. Do not let failures discourage you, try again. Be happy whenever there is the slightest call for it. When you accept yourself as you are, it will be easier for you to accept other people.

Be worthy of your humanity and your human rights.

Anneli Hakala, 18, Finland

If your friend is hungry or thirsty,
Give him your share.
If your friend is in want of love,
Love him.
If your friend is in want of home and clothes,
Give him a cottage and clothes.
If your friend is lonely,
Keep him company.
If your friend is lying,
Silence him.
If your friend calls to you,
Listen to him.
If your friend is laughing,
Laugh with him.
If your friend is crying,
Cry with him.
If your friend is ill,
Fetch help.
If your friend dies,
Don't forget him.

Paula Lagerstam, 15, Finland

We children have often heard from grownups in recent years that kids nowadays cannot even sharpen a pencil with their knife or tie their shoestrings. The reason why we can't do these things is not because we are lazy. It is because there are too many modern conveniences around. And so, we are not trained to do these things, even though we should have learned them in our childhood.

In my family we have two parakeets. Since their birth the parakeets had been fed peeled millet seeds, and so when I recently gave them unpeeled millet seeds, they kicked them away and ate nothing. They merely flapped their wings with much irritation, as their food box was filled and their stomach was still empty.

I don't want to be like the parakeets. By reading lots of books, building up my physical strength, or doing my utmost at what I am supposed to do in my childhood, I wish to improve my native capabilities. When inventors, discoverers, and men with technical and political ability are reared, a society of peace, prosperity, and happiness will be born. Only after this will there be a rise in the general standard of living of the people.

Takaaki Suzuki, 12, Japan

Often when I lie in bed many thoughts push into my mind and keep me awake, especially when I have been watching TV or when I have heard on the radio nothing but bad news: fighting between Christians and Moslems, guerrilla-war in Rhodesia, racial conflicts in South Africa; hi-jacking somewhere in Europe, starvation in South America and India, crimes and accidents everywhere.

About one million people vegetate in prisons and in lunatic asylums because of their religious or political conviction. This is the world we live in today. Every 9th minute a person starves to death whereas we have a surplus of food; this is the world we are responsible for.

The more I hear things like that, the more I get restless, the more I wish to live in a world of peace and security, in a world where all people love each other, trust each other, help each other.

But isn't it an illusion, a utopia to think that a better world will come true? Is it really true that I can do nothing against the evil in the world? I am just one and there are about 4 milliards of people . . . But what if *I* really start getting better and if I try to make *other* young people think what they could do to change their environment?

Yet to be good isn't always easy. It means: forget yourself, help other people, be kind to your parents, be patient to your sisters and brothers, listen to the talking of the old people, show them that you love them and will help them a little. How many opportunities are there at school? And again it isn't easy to become a good student without being a pusher. When I am grown up, I must have the courage to speak in favour of people who suffer from injustice. I must try to become a good daughter, a good sister, a good wife, a good mother, a good neighbour, in a word – a good woman.

And when I have a family of my own, all members, my husband, my children should be accepted in love; they must really feel they are beloved and trusted. I will treat them with all my love and yet with firmness. I know only loved people are able to love again.

Later at school my children must learn to cooperate with foreign pupils, they must learn to accept and respect them as they are. In the small communities we are put in – you and I and even my little children – we can build a better world.

No one is allowed to withdraw. We must engage. May be one of us feels a special vocation to take care of old or sick people, to help physically impaired children – don't hesitate, help! Make them believe that people accept them in spite of their old age and their defects.

If we all want to do some good actions – a chain reaction will start and the dream of a better world will become reality at least at one end of the world.

Halbmayr Gertraud, 17, Austria

I would like to go to Africa or the Near East to do what I can to help those in need.

I am rather doubtful at this stage whether I will be mature enough when I am grown-up to leave this safe and comfortable world of mine to hurry to a strange world to struggle to get the same rights to the people there which I have been able to enjoy.

Am I just a girl dreaming of being a kind of heroine who leaves the civilized world to ease the life of some people who are totally strange to her? I don't think so, Even as a little girl I remember having thought that when I grow up I could go and help others. The work I have in mind would require strength, I would have to give up many comforts. But it would also give a lot of satisfaction, I would have to do with people and above all, I would learn to value things differently.

Let's hope that I have the stamina to realise my aim to make a better world.

Kirsi Rahikainen, 15, Finland

I must do for my country not to wait every day and say, what will my country do for me.

Keipone Kebapetse, 14, Botswana

You and I make up this world and to make it right we first have to make ourselves right.

We have to respect each other. Respect each other so much that no dictator can force us to destroy one another. We must not waste our lives, believing that our successors will put the world right for us.

Ladan Rafū, 14, Iran

I CAN HELP TOO

Fitzroy Solomon, 15, Jamaica

Veronica

My village is found in Eastern of St Catherine. It is about two square miles and though not hilly is found between two hills. It is a beautiful little village and is liked by its inhabitants. Visitors like to take picture of the beautiful scenery to take away for rememberance. But all its beauty it has problems.

My village has no electricity and no proper irrigation. Many building needs reabilitations. It has no market to save the people from going great distance to sell their food. The other thing it needs is a recreation training centre for the youths.

Most of the youths in my village just idle their time away now. But some are doing bad things like stealing. They cannot find anything better to occupy their time. Building a recreation training centre would change them greatly. They would have something important to do. Those are the thing I would do to solve the problems of my village. It would be more beautiful.

Veronica Tomlinson,
Jamaica

How to set right the world? First I will examine myself how I am in the house with brother and sisters and parents. I must correct myself. I must be honest and helpful in the house. If there are animals, I must take care of them with kindness. I must be an example to the neighbours. Second the village or town where I live. First I must make a team of children of my age and tell them how we should be helpful in the house, school and with other elders. If I live in a place where there are different people with different languages, I will try to learn the language. Language must be a link with neighbours. Learn as many languages as possible. If the state gets right, the country gets right. There must be give and take policy of foodgrains, oil and aids to science and industry. I must make people understand that hard labour in field, cattle and poultry farms are necessary to keep the world alive. Seek peace and not hatred. Give respect and take respect. Whatever a country has in bulk, share that with other countries which need. My conclusion is I must be right to help put the world right.

Rajendran Nagalingam, 13, India

Babatunde Williams, 10, Nigeria

114

I can put the world right by giving the poor food, money, clothes and shelter. Some people have children suffering with hunger. Maybe I can give them food to make them happy. People are thirsty. I can save up some money to give the Government to pay some men to pump for water. If people are dying and have to go to the hospital, I can be a nurse when I grow up to save the peoples lives. Gastro sometimes go around because of flies and mosquitoes. I can keep the place clean by picking up the rubbish, burning it and sweeping it.

Elizabeth Lum Kin, 8, Trinidad

Do your work so that your employer can rely on you and see to it that everyone gets an employment. We must educate even our little children to do their work and duties exactly and patiently. When they are grown up everybody can rely on them.

Gabriele Kleindl, 17, Austria

If everyone just did his bit, the world would be wonderful. But the people always want things ready on a silver plate, without exerting any efforts. I am one of those who dream, but I have just one slight difference, and this is that I try to do something about it. I've got a lot of dreams. Some may appear serious and very good and some may appear childish and even funny. I'd like to share some of them with you, dear reader. Who knows? Someday, when I grow up, I may be able to make some of my dreams if not all come true. One of the greatest dreams I have and am trying to realize is to help people. I would love to be a doctor and help find a cure for cancer. Who knows, maybe I become the one who saves millions of people. This is the greatest of my dreams. If all people feel this way, and try to do something to improve this world, if each one of us does his small or big part in life, this world would not be a world any more but it will rather be a paradise.

Randa Risgallah, 14, Egypt

We need more tidy people. On just about every sweet paper it says 'KEEP BRITAN TIDY', hardly any body takes any notice. There should be more bins. I can make them. I'm going to dot them about round our village.

Susan Strike,
United Kingdom

Dear Reader,
This land consolidation is the only thing which make most of the troubles in the world today. In the ancient time you can go anywhere in your country, and built your home there. Today you cannot do this, WHY?
Nobody is the owner of any land what so ever. God is the owner of land and he made it for people not for one person in the world. Thank you God bless you.
Yours Lovely
Fredrick

Fredrick Otieno, Kenya

Elizabeth Lum Kin

Fredrick Otieno

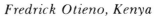

Can I tell you? It is too difficult to put the world right. I would rather try to put right some crooked boys in my neighbourhood.

Christos Alexakis, 8, Greece

Antoinette Bishop

Maurer Ulrike

Thinking of the past makes me sometimes sad; thinking of the future alarms me and yet I like dreaming of how we could put the world right.
I think of the smallest community, of the family. There we start our lives; in the first years of our lives the character is formed. The life in the family is decisive for the future of the children. If they were loved and trusted, if they could feel the warmness of a mother heart, the love and firmness of a good father, they couldn't become so inhuman and merciless in later life. If even little children were respected by their parents they would learn to be respectful to others.
Parents and teachers must be sensible enough to let a child grow at his own pace and allow time for daydreaming and stargazing.
If education could continue in this way I think young people must become kind and good. It's never too early to help them distinguish between good and evil, to become critical, to make their own decisions, to obey their conscience.
I know from my own experience that this demands sacrifices, it's not a comfortable life. And as people have their own free will they also can choose the evil and that's why the world will never be entirely good.
But if you and I and many of us, try to do our best the world must become better — at least at one end.

Maurer Ulrike, 16, Austria

Hyacinth D Griffith, 11, Barbados

Mr (or Ms) Anybody agrees that brotherly love must be promoted among all men of whatever race, colour, creed or class, if world-wide peace is to be a reality; yet how can man expect this world tolerance if he finds it necessary to be more polite, considerate and patient towards someone he meets at a friend's home, than towards his immediate family. If this courtesy could be spread to the family circle, there would be fewer cases of broken homes, alcoholism, drug addiction and overweight (yes, overweight!), in this world, to mention only a few of its ills. Then there is the man who despises terms such as 'working class, middle class, upper class', and thinks they are an insult to mankind, but explains to his son, at great length, why he should not marry the trash-collector's daughter.
We constantly tell each other that we must learn to share the grief of others and rejoice for their happiness, so we are willing to support a poverty-striken family. But when rich and pretty Jackie Onassis' name is slandered throughout the corners of every island and continent after her second husband's death, we make no pretence of not being joyful — after all, why must *she* have all the luck!
Mr Know-It-All and his wife compose a petition stating that people of all races must be given a fair deal; but listen to the lady and her friends categorise Mrs Know-It-All's cousin with the 34-24-34 figure as a shallow, conceited flirt, while Mr Know-It-All explains that his 'best friend' managed to buy a huge Spanish-styled house by 'toadying-up to the boss'.
It is hard, but it would be easier on the soul and face (unkind thoughts mould an unkind face), if we all developed the will-power to abstain from these exciting character-blasting sessions.
If this world is to be improved, work must start immediately and in the home. Be as considerate and cheery towards your little brother as you are for the old man you help across the road, pay parents the respect due to them, and *think* before you relate what you 'heard about Janice'. Consider *your* faults before you let loose.

Sheridan Reece, 16, Barbados

The family is the centre — the family where all the members, children and growns up, can express their ideas with respect, freedom and love. The families in a neighbourhood should work together in running various social services: for example the local school. Everyone young and old should have a place and everyone should feel united for the common good.

Anna Maline Potrizie, Italy

Now to me, talk is cheap, and preaching love to mankind seems to be all in vain. For I really don't think it is fair for parents and leaders to preach love, and then they go and do the opposite.

Now most older people might think that the younger generation coming up today is too hostile against their elders, but do they honestly know that it really isn't our fault? If a child hasn't been shown love at home by his elders, he is doomed to hate and frustration.

For when, and only when, a child is taught and shown what real love is from his parents and home, can he then go out into the world and show his own little friends what real love is.

Now I'm not saying that this method would solve the big problem of war, but I'm just trying to say it might help the problem in a small way. For war really comes from the source of hatred towards one another and the selfish feelings most of us entertain.

Antoinette Bishop, Barbados

When, and only when, a child is shown real love from his parents can he go into the world and show his own little friends what real love is.

Antoinette Bishop, Barbados

We should be kind to people and help people when they need it. When we put flowers in the garden we should care for them and water them so they are healthy. When you have friends you should play fair and everyone should like everyone in the world and don't say you hate people just by their looks. You should take care of your pets and everyone in your family you should love especialy your Mum and Dad. You should not kick or hurt knowone. Be kind to everyone.

Barbara Webb, 9, Australia

Efiok E Efiok, 10, Nigeria

Life is full of beautiful and horrible things. He who is lucky gains rest, peace, comfort, and happiness in it; and he who is bitterly stung by life's misfortunes, curses it and demands more of it. With all its fortunes and misfortunes, life is simply lovely; too sweet to be given up.

But not everyone can understand what life is, what one's value in life is. A very few people look into their lives and try to find a moral in it. They look carefully into events and try to deduce the precious purpose of existence. The majority of people go on hurting other people's feelings, losing their temper at silly things, and losing their time for nothing as though they were made to live a billion years. They are blown by the current of events in life. Their life begins and ends as it began. Some people leave deep marks on life and can never be forgotten after their death; while others leave life and are quickly forgotten like a breeze that passes quickly by.

Some people are candles that burn in complete darkness. Some people are handicapped but they become great because they have faith in themselves and God. Courage is being able to think and act even when the worst happens. Some people are eighty and ninety years old but they are still youthful. They are youthful with their ideas, production, and creative work. They love life and they give it as much as they take from it, and maybe more.

Bahiga Abed, 16, Egypt

To God, the Creator of the world
from a humble creation, me,
the world,
in the Solar System,
On Earth,
in Asia,
Iran,
in a house,
a corner of
Shemiran.
Dear God,
There is war,
There is hunger,
There is bloodshed, murder, death.
O, love and Peace,
And faith and goodness,
what is left?
If I were you,
the mighty Creator of the world,
I'd put no boundary line,

No land named country,
Nothing.
So, everyone,
And every single man,
O white and black,
And red and yellow,
could live in peace and love,
and share their joy and sorrow,
and plough the land,
and give the grain to everyone.

Mojgan Pooya, 12, Iran

Nuffield School for the Deaf & Blind
Sri Lanka

Honourable President Carter,
Happy Xmas and a prosperous New Year to you and the people of your country. I wanted to send you a greeting card, but later I decided I would write a letter because I have so many news to write you and I can't inform them to you in a greeting card. President Carter on the 20th December I went out with my father on a Xmas shopping to Town. I had to buy a new frock for me. I am 14 years old, and so I am grown up. I have reached up the height of the shoulders of my mother you see!

Oh! I have forgotton the main point I wanted to write. The Town was nothing but an array of shining stars. All the shops were illuminated and everywhere there were beautiful dolls and frocks and flowers and what not. President Carter, I bought a cream frock with laces all over the neck and shoulder. There was cream buttons also on the frock.

After the shopping we went to the biggest hotel in the town and had ice-cream, and icing cake. I love ice-cream President Carter. My stomach was full and I was too happy with everything. Just as we crossed the road I saw a boy of my age with lame legs and an egg shape body lying on the pavement with his mother. Oh! I simply can't describe how I felt to see the lame boy. Since that boy cannot understand my sign language, I asked my father who can understand my sign language as to why that boy is like that. He said he is a deformed child. At once I remembered my teacher teaching in class, why and how these deformities take place. She told us that after the World War the entire atmosphere is polluted and that it affects gradually the children in the mother's womb.

Could it be that is why I am also defective in my hearing? My mother is making baby frocks in pink and blue colour and she told me to expect the

Funsho Speaking to President J. Carter U.S.A.
J. Carter U.S.A.   Funsho

Funsho Farinre, 9, Nigeria

Funsho Farinre

Bahiga Abed

Ukkarista

Funsho:
Mr President, I know you can help me, because you are older and wiser than I am.

Pres:
Yes Funsho, but what can I do for you?

Funsho:
Now, I am the Ruler of my country Nigeria, and soon I will be the Ruler of the world. In my country we have many poor people, and many rich people also. How can I make the rich help the poor, and give them some of their money?

Pres:
That will not be easy, but as you are the Ruler, your people will listen to you. Call all the rich, and tell them, of the poor, who have no food, no houses, no clothes. They will be ashamed if a young child talks to them. And I think they will help their own people.

Funsho:
If I tell them you help me, they would be ashamed and must help us.

Pres:
Yes I think so I will send you machines for the farmers, builders to make houses, schools, hospitals and also some money to start with.

Funsho:
Oh thank you Mr. President, you are very kind. I shall tell all my people, how you want to help us, and they must also say a big thank you. We hope our dear country Nigeria, will then be a great country like the United States of America.

arrival of a small sister or brother soon. I am very sorry to think that such a defect like lame leg and yellow colour can come to my little brother or sister also.
I hate all these wars President Carter! Why are people fighting? Please give them enough food, new frocks and beautiful houses, and ask them not to fight with bomb and all. We don't want lame legged and yellow coloured children with egg shape body. Their mothers will be unhappy.
Thank you, I have forgotten to tell you that I have bought a beautiful doll too.
Yours sincerely
Ukkarista
Ukkarista Soosaipillai, Sri Lanka

119

I'm alive in my little universe and I strive as much as I can to do my best and to satisfy those who trust me.

I'm carried away by the trend of my simple life, of my minor problems, and the moments when I can speak to myself are very few. But there are some moments when, escaping from this tumult, I looked around and I feel deeply disappointed and dissatisfied. The stream of my thoughts comes back to reality, stirred by pieces of information in a newspaper. I have always had the feeling that behind all these figures and cold statistics there is something deeper, more serious, and then with my eyes of my mind I try to think of that corner of the world in the fragment of information in a column of a daily paper. I summarize in my mind everything I learned about misery, poverty and starvation, suffering and war — only notions for me — and I try to turn them into consistent images. But, oh, the most important element is missing: experience.

I can't write about what those men feel, do, or think, because I didn't live in such a world. But, I can write and I *will* write about what I feel for those who experience this cruel reality without being helped to get out of their situation.

It's difficult for me to have the image of a child who didn't feel the caress of his parents or the charming smile of his happy mother. I can't imagine parents giving birth to children with only the feeling of remorse, that they brought into this world another slave of suffering. But I know that this world exists and will exist as long as people spin round little problems of their own interests, as long as they expect just immediate profits.

We, the youth, who received the relay-race, we want a better world and we know there is no mistake in wanting it. I know the Earth is everything we have, it is most valuable in the universe. We stretched our hand up to the Moon, we strive to reach Mars but the Earth, good or bad, is where we belong.

Boeru Daniela Lucia, 13, Romania

120

If she would ever be in danger, I'm sure that any problem is going to find a real solution and then there is no point in differences of colour, religion or any other border. Then we shall feel, all of us, the whole pain of mankind, and maybe then we shall understand that each of us has the same heart, that everyone asks his right for a better life, that all of us raise in despair to save our world.

We are living now the century of repeated mistakes.

We have the experience when the pillars of the civilization had been overturned, when Shakespeare, Goethe, Balzac, Tolstoi had lost the cheers and the air roared in the honour of men whose originality was in the cut and colour of the shirt and the glorious boots suggesting the crushing of culture. We had the rusted taste of the war and then we began a 'cold' one. We stock thousands of millions of dollars in bombs and crush the world under the weight of useless equipment; we sharpen again the pencils for war-accounts.

No, this is really too much, we don't want any more. We want the cordial noise of peace, not the reckless whistle of the siren.

What the scientists hatch in some labs seems to me a sinister work. There are odious deliriums in the name of care for civilization; even if we admit that these horrors could be discovered — like a substance which can burn an entire town instantly — we must find men to hide the dangerous toys from the lunatics who are lured to play with them.

Not one of these acute problems can be solved studying an A-bomb.

It seems curious to me that having the experience of the past, and of its consequences, we are inclined just to discuss, and have a feeling of security and the temptation of dozing-off in this situation.

It's horrible that the atomic and cybernetic age keeps these residues of an age of ignorance and violence; truth is still neglected — checked by an entire history. People can't be subjected with the force of the weapon or dictatorship. It's said that if we are going to continue in the same way the fourth confrontation between us will be with the club and the stone. It's strange for me that the people think now of the fourth confrontation. Oh men, the most important thing is not to get to the third one.

Alongside fighting against pollution of the water, of the soil, or the air, we must fight against the pollution of relations between people and states. For many years Africa meant for me just tom-toms, bananas and jungle. That's what I knew when I stopped from the whirl of films. I wiped off the colour of photos and I opened at the first page the history of the Black Continent. The continent blacked by sufferings and bitterness, tossing in the black oceans of despair, scorched under the black tears rolled in the desert. We forget what brightness and colour, what strength, we lose in this world. No, this world is not the best. We stake too much on people's patience — forgetting that each of us has a right to a better life.

We the youth can't stay out of this. I'm conscious that the best or the brightest ability is worthless if those who have it are incapable of integrating it in a general action. We must gather our forces and cultivate the taste for love and freedom, to fight with all the power on an intellectual front to win the peace, because what we have now is a threat to our nights of rest and days of work. Like real dockers, who work in the port where the ideas arrive, we should refuse the unloading of the war-cry!

Rădulescu Cristina, 18, Romania

Hello all of you, — people of the world. Please listen to me, no matter what your age, race or creed; I want you to listen to what I have to say, because it is of the utmost importance and concerns us all. It is simply, 'The world is in a *MESS*!!' and I add that 'It is all mankind's fault!' Hey, don't stop reading and run off now; I knew you wouldn't appreciate hearing that, but I had to say it anyway because it is *true!* I am not only speaking of the physical wrong which we have brought on our planet earth — errors like pollution and the breaking down of the ozone layer; or the indiscriminate hunting of some animals which has led to the falling through of nature's food chain of the wild. What I am speaking of, mainly, are the wrongs man has brought through his selfishness, greed and cruelty.

Think what a wonderful world it would be if people did not think all the time of themselves but thought instead of how they could give a little happiness through thoughtful little actions, like opening a door for an old lady or buying a little child — even if he is a stranger — a piece of candy. Doing things like that doesn't take a lot out of you, but shows that you care for other people and people like to know that someone, even a total stranger, cares. However, the world is so full of corruption now that even these little kindnesses are viewed with distrust. The old person thinks you want to pick his pocket or 'mug' him (most likely someone has already done this before to him, or one of his friends). The little child has been warned by his mother never to accept anything from a stranger.

Above all I believe that in order to make this a really wonderful world we need wisdom to control our thoughts and actions, and wisdom is not a flower to be picked but a mountain to be climbed.

So we must strive to climb this mountain in order to be free from evil, for evil cannot be conquered in the world but only resisted within one's self. If we all can resist it, we will have 'conquered' it in the world.

Love to you all,

Sally Harris, 15, Barbados

Please answer before I burst

Dear Leaders of Nations,
To what destination are you leading us to — Heaven or Hell? Do you still remember how green places used to be? Your great grandchildren will have the 'privilege' of everyday contact with the concrete jungle. Instead of the natural clouds, they shall see clouds of smog. Why do you want to give your dirty smoke to the Heavens? What ARE you up to? Are you NEVER satisfied? And furthermore, you go to the moon and stick your flag up there as if the moon were your own. Very soon, you'll be calling the moon your next State. You have space link-ups and shake hands with your so-called friends (on earth you are enemies). Why can't you have healthier relationships here on earth? Instead of wasting money to multiply your 'wealth', why don't you help feed, clothe and shelter the thousands, nay, millions, who lack basic necessities? Instead of building more and more skyscrapers, why can't you build small and hygienic cottages for the poor?
At a time when we are in grave need of peace and anti-pollution steps we see an irresponsible country 'bombarding' in the Pacific. (Thank God they've stopped now.) They are showing to the world how 'powerful' they are. Yes, you are indeed getting more powerful. One of these days, you'll be building castles in the air with corpses.
I now fully agree with Havelock Ellis' saying: 'What we call progress is the exchange of one nuisance for another nuisance'.
One country has progressed so much in two hundred years that it has poisoned at least five lakes with its industrial wastes. May I congratulate them?
Are you leaders leading yourself and others, especially the innocent ones, to a world of peace or are you driving the world to pieces? Peace be with you if you are doing the former. And may you be condemned if you're doing the latter. Please answer my queries before I burst.
I shall remain (if you don't help me) A frustrated and disillusioned youngster,

Mathi Azhagu, Fiji

Dear World,
Military analyst Ranson W. Baldwin calculated that in some 3,457 years of recorded history, there have been more than 3,230 years of war and only 227 years of peace. Even now in many different places war rages — in the East, North, South and West. On all continents and for differing reasons. People, our world is on a drastic course, leading to self-destruction. It is a car speeding 200kph along a narrow pot-holed road leading to a cliff edge. You must all join forces to stop this car.

You are destroying yourselves and the system by your ambitious striving for materialistic things. True it is nice to have food, clothing, shelter and secure jobs. But once secure, why must you still seek? Why not give to the hungry? You know we are all imperfect beings. We all get sick and eventually die. We are mortal. We can't turn ourselves into immortal beings.

We all look for peace and security, don't we? Can men bring it? Can the U.N.? They have a statue showing a man beating a sword into a ploughshare; 'And the nations will have to beat their swords into ploughshares and their spears into pruning shears. Nations will not lift up sword against nation, neither will they learn war any more'. The U.N. has not been able to stop war and the ever-increasing awareness that war involves everyone has created tension, strain and problems among world leaders.

Don't become cowards. True we live in an era evoking fear, but try to do something to help. Don't contribute more problems to an already burdened world. Make this world a world you'd like your child to grow up in.

You are a child of the Universe, no less than the trees and the stars.
You have a right to be here, and whether or not it is clear to you the Universe is unfolding as it should ...
With all its sham and drudgery it is still a beautiful world.
Be careful. Strive to be happy.
'Desiderata'

I leave it to you now. Help one another, care for one another, but most of all, love one another. We're all brothers, so treat each other as brothers. Join forces now to make sorrow and pain a thing of the past, and happiness a thing of the present and future.
Love always,
Tania Wolfgramm, 14, Tonga

Are you so blind?

Dear World,
Yes, you are sick and tired of all the suffering.

But are you so blind? Don't you realise that it is you and you only, each and every individual that makes up our world, that is responsible and no one is any more to blame than the next person?

Face this fact with braveness and boldness; our world is falling apart. Now is not the time to despair and sigh but the time to get out and help your neighbours.

The world in which we are now living is crazy, mixed up and confused. The world's course is like that of a runaway train, speeding downhill toward a yawning canyon, the bridge over which has been washed out. Does that shock you? Let's face it. You've known for a long time.

In his book 'Future Shock', Alven Toffler writes: 'We are simultaneously experiencing a youth revolution, a sexual revolution, a racial revolution, a colonial revolution and the most rapid and deep-going technological revolution in history'.

Because of this, we cannot blame youth for everything they do. It is they that are affected most as they are about to gain power in the world. We must try to grasp the effect that the shocking revolution has had upon youth. A youth may exclaim: 'How dare the parents use up all the resources, pollute the environment, ruin everything. What about us? What is there we have to offer our children?' What have you to say, older generation? Ha! You turn away, or say how ungrateful youth is. What about the fact that never before has a generation of young people grown up with knowledge of nuclear weapons and their ability to wipe out civilisation several times over?

When I started to write this letter, I did not have in mind telling you all how wonderful you were, nor did I want to talk about living in a fairy-tale world where people would live in bubbles floating far above the clouds without a care. No, I wanted everyone to know about the world in which they now live. It's real, it's alive but it's dying. It is up to us — all of us — to change it.

Ruth Wolfgramm, 16, Tonga

Dalia Haver, Israel

I hope year two thousand will give
  us an Earth
No longer squeaking and groaning
  under a planetful of arms.
I hope for the day when Dad and
  Mum will take baby by the hand
Lead him to the War Museum there
  to contemplate and shudder at
The last weapon on Earth — the
  man-made, man-eating monster
Gnawing ineffectually at the cage
  made of the
Timelessly strong alloy of
  PEACE & BROTHERHOOD OF
  MAN.

Capra Victor, 15, Romania

Windows
(A letter to an extra-terrestrial friend)

'There are thousands of thousands
  of windows here on planet Earth.
Some windows are of exquisite
  Murano flint-glass,
Others are just poor shows
  of ordinary glass.
And against the falling night,
on this here planet, my friend
it looks as though every window,
each pane of glass
is part of a soul
opened like a water-lily cup
towards infinity …

A thought is then budding inside me,
a thought that each atom of soul
  portends eyes for me,
whether blue, black or
  emerald-green
they all reveal one word,
the looks of all eyes unite
like a milky shadow of stars
and the warm and clear air rings
with the same divinely echoed word:
Pace, Peace, Paix, Pax, Frieden,
  Mir …'

A child of this old-old Earth
and several other millions like him.
Sever Mircea Avram, 17, Romania

Big and small, happy, smiling children
all over the world! This is your friend
from Poland. I think that you live with
each other as brothers, without
quarrels and play together and help
each other to do your homework. I
know that there will come a day when
all of the children in the world will
meet, shake hands and say, 'Long live
peace!'

Iwona Myszko, 15, Poland

Medardo Hernandes, 12, Honduras

If the whole world had peace everyone would stay happly, because peace is the mother of everything.

Farasten Kadgunge, Rhodesia

Look!
A white dove is flying!
Its wings are shining
with the pure brightness of freedom!
Oh, dear world,
Be kind and good,
And don't smear or break
My pure dove's wings!

Look!
A white dove is flying hopefully
criss-crossing the clear-blue skies,
skies clear-blue like a maiden's eyes.
Oh, peoples of my mother planet,
Do cherish the maiden's blue-skied
  look!

And please do look once more
to see the white dove fly
and look trustingly to you.
Please don't
grieve her wee little heart,
and help her fly more graciously,
more quietly
more daringly . . .

Frangulea Daniela, 15, Romania

My example comes from house flies, they fly all the time, eat all the time, mate all the time, and are dying all the time, but these house flies are harmless to one another. They fly together, eat together, drink together. There is no king to rule others and they are always happy. They cry the same. If only people can speak together, drink together, work together, stay together and speak one language. All these added together would keep world peace together. Colour may be colour only without any significance at all, we are black and clever no matter what a white, yellow, brown or red man can do we are capable. If we are 'Baboons' of course, you always see Baboons together peacefully and laughing and that shows that they know something in their heavenlet, I mean small heaven. Peace to the world, to everyone, harmony to our world.

Buzzord Goaletson, Botswana

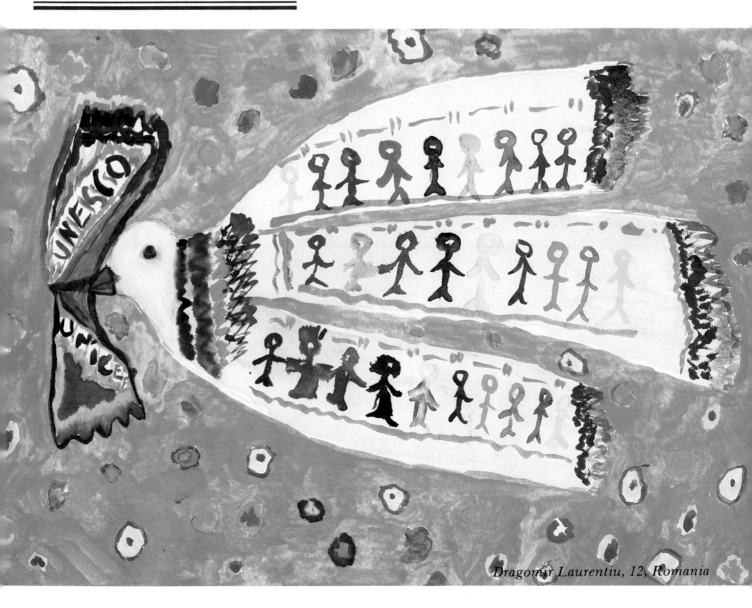

Dragomir Laurentiu, 12, Romania

I ponder sometimes and try to see
Far into the future, what I want to
  behold
When my children are young. When I
  am old
How different or indifferent will that
  era be?

Who can expect everybody to love
  everyone?
I don't expect it. But, what I do expect
Is respect, deep, sincere and true
  respect.
The proper deference that no man is
  below or above.

And yet, I don't want a perfect world
  for my children.
I want a world which they themselves
  will be able to perfect
And shape it to the needs which they
  themselves select.
With one for all, and all for one
  prospective end.

I want my children to grow up in a
  world
Where all at least try to love
  their neighbours as themselves
Where honesty and peace are not
  shoved upon shelves
To grow dusty, disfigured and old.

For every human holds a part of the
  world in his hands
He helps to decide his own era's future.
He paints but a minute part of the
  picture
But one blot! And you can't tell
  sea from land.

Cheryl Harris, 13, Barbados

I would like a world, a very beautiful
  world,
Somewhat like this one for my
  children.
A world of peace,
  love and happiness,
A world of comfort and joy.

I would like a world, a very beautiful
  world,
Somewhat like this one, for my
  children.
A world of flowers, beautiful flowers
  all over.

Jennifer Brown, 14, Jamaica

Now that I am a young lady and almost prepared to have my sons I will try to guide them to choose a world of comfort where they can study and prepare themselves for the future.
I will guide my children to look for a world without selfishness, without poverty and hunger. I will teach them to help needy persons and love those who don't care for themselves.
The most beautiful thing in the world is that my children will know that their mother wishes the best for them. I will feel proud and happy knowing that my children have found in this world comfort and happiness after a great effort in the past years.
My children will be an example for me and for mankind.

*Martha Celsa Amador, 16, Honduras
(Orphan in Oxfam-supported S O S
Children's Village.)*

I wish that my children would be able to live in a more peaceful world with no wars, no pollution. One would hope that nature were clean and beautiful, the people natural, free and happy living in harmony with nature, animals and their surroundings. In my world people would live in small, beautiful houses with few families living together. Everybody should have a garden, flowers, vegetables and space to move. One would hope for safe streets with no fear of being assaulted, robbed or disturbed. Schools and jobs would be pleasant places where people would be glad to go. The teachers might have more time for their pupils to instruct and teach them in a friendly and individual way. The people's born talent and special gifts would perhaps come forth more easily, they might sing, draw, paint and move more willingly. But above all, the people would not quarrel. Envy, hatred and unnatural competition and rivalry would be unnecessary. People would be accepted as such. Nobody would be discriminated because of illness, colour, language, religion, place of birth, sex or any such reason.
This is the world I should hope for my children — if only it were possible.

Sini-Kirsi Kehravuo, 19, Finland

I would hate to see my children crippled or hungry or cold while others are living happily and safely in other countries.

Sami Raghda, 15, Egypt

126

Ratan, 12, India

I would like my children to live in a calm country with peace. The country free from quarrels, the country where everybody feels free, the country where wanderers may get shelter.

Mpeo Seroto, 13, Lesotho

In a way I am afraid of the future. It has been said that there will be no food, there will be a new Ice Age, there will be big earthquakes. And what's more, there is the fear of the Third World War.

I would like to know that my children can live in a safe world where they do not have to experience war or to starve. I hope that they will be able to live in a world which offers everybody a sufficient living, in a world where all people are equal, in a world where people would be friends with each other and happy. I would also like to know that our descendants could see clean nature. I would also like to see overpopulation being solved and industrial countries helping developing countries.

I would like every country to have its independence and the freedom to decide its own affairs. I would like every country to be democratic so that people could freely express their opinions without having to be afraid of losing their lives.

Sirpa Pasula, 15, Finland

Bengali text (top):

কনাকে উড় করে দিয়ে মেঘের রাজ্যেতে
বে, পাহাড়ের চূড়ায় নেচে নেচে ঘুরে
ড়িবো। বনার- জলে গাভাসি যে স্রোতে
যে ছেয়ে সব পাহাড় থেকে পাহাড়ে
রাবো। মানুষ গ্রহ প্রহীনুরে যাবে
ওতি নেবে ঘুরে বেড়াবে নূতন মানুষের।

MoFoKA STD6 15th November Ghomane Primary school, Years old

Bonhelo 000 ke lakaletsang bana bat ka.
lakaletsa bana bu ka bophelo bo botle bo monate,
rutehe ho lekana mehla ea joale, ba tle ba tsoele haha
bona molemo, hape ke lakaletsa ha bana ba ka ba
nhela bophelo ba bo kreste e be batho ba tsepahalang
amahong, lipuong le liketsong e be bana ba ratang l
no ba tletseng mosa le lerato sechabeng sa habo.

دنیا کا فلاح - میرا خواب

نہ تو میں بادشاہ ہوں اور نہ نظامہر میرے بادشاہ بن جانے کے امکانات موجود ہیں
میرے ذہن کے ویران اور تاریک گوشوں میں کبھی ایک خیال جھلتا ہے اور شرارے کا طلو
نانا فنا ہو جاتا ہے کہ دنیا کا ہمہ مقتدر شخصیت ہوں تو ان تمام کوتاہیوں اور برائی
شتاب کرسکوں گا جن کوتاہیوں اور برائیوں نے انسانیت کو دنیی اعضوں اور روحا
اکساتھ ساتھ معاشی ملوک العالی میں مبتلا کر رکھا ہے ۔

EL MUNDO Si yo fuera gobernador del mundo quisiera Fa
e fuera así. Yo quisiera que el mundo estuviera lleno
felicidad no hubiera miseria, hambre, crimen y gamines.
siera que hubiera educacion para todo niño. Pero para llegar

Right margin (English):
You and
world ar
we first
ourselves
We have
other.
Respect
much th
force us
another.

Ve
B

Right margin (Dutch):
Iedereen
weet
OOK
WAARO
DOE je

Je
al
Ha
Po
de
O